Handbook for Authors

of Papers in
American Chemical
Society Publications

AMERICAN CHEMICAL SOCIETY

WASHINGTON, D. C.   1978

Library of Congress CIP Data

American Chemical Society.
Handbook for authors.
Edition of 1965 published under title: Handbook for
authors of papers in the research journals of the Amer-
ican Chemical Society; ed. of 1967 published under title:
Handbook for authors of papers in the journals of the
American Chemical Society.

Bibliography: p.
Includes index.

1. Technical writing. 2. Report writing. I. Title.
T11.A4 1978 808′.025 78-6401

ISBN 0-8412-0425-X
ISBN 0-8412-0430-6 pbk.   1–122   1978

Contents

Foreword

It has been 10 years since the first edition of the American Chemical Society "Handbook for Authors" was published—years in which technological promises in composition became realities, and innovations became standard procedures. The production of scientific journals, as indeed of most printed material, is now part of the computer age.

Whereas those of us who are familiar with and admire the craftsmanship that produced our publications in the past view its passing with nostalgia, we who are involved in scientific information transfer welcome the possibilities inherent in modern technology and have learned to appreciate the different type of craftsmanship that is part of the publication production system today.

This edition of the "Handbook for Authors" differs from the previous one in small but important ways: it reflects changes in nomenclature, symbolism, and terminology that have been adopted internationally or nationally in the intervening years; it recommends a format for reference citations that approaches an ACS-wide standard; it discusses the limitations of and problems inherent in current composition systems; and it addresses areas in which further technological improvements would affect manuscript preparation.

Despite the many small, detailed changes called for, an author's overall approach to manuscript preparation itself has really not changed. Thus, this guide incorporates much of the same advice and general information that was present in the first edition. It is our hope that it will be an effective aid to new authors as well as a useful companion to more experienced writers.

No foreword to the culmination of so much organization and hard work would be complete without recording the debt of gratitude owed to Dr. Marianne Brogan, Associate Head of the Editorial Department in the Books and Journals Division. Dr. Brogan shepherded the entire revision project from the very beginning. Dr. Brogan received much assistance and advice from many other people within and without the ACS and they are duly recognized in the Acknowledgments, but in many real ways this handbook is her work.

D. H. Michael Bowen, Director
Books and Journals Division
American Chemical Society

Acknowledgments

Throughout the revision of this handbook I have received constant encouragement, criticism, and advice from my colleagues in the Books and Journals and Chemical Abstracts Service Divisions of the American Chemical Society, from the editors of the Society's journals, and from fellow members of the American Chemical Society Committee on Nomenclature. They in turn have solicited advice from and encouraged me to consult members of the academic, industrial, societal, and government communities on various topics discussed in this guide. To all of them I express my gratitude.

Marianne Brogan
Editorial Department

I. AMERICAN CHEMICAL SOCIETY BOOKS AND JOURNALS

The publications program of the American Chemical Society ranges from primary journals to secondary services, from monographs to magazines, from reprint collections to symposia, from biography to state-of-the-art presentations. This guide is designed primarily as an aid to those authors who plan to submit manuscripts to the journals published by the American Chemical Society and to those who participate in book publication projects. A prospective contributor to any of these publications should also consult recent issues for content, style, specific recommendations, and criteria.

A brief outline of the scope of each journal and special book series follows.

ACCOUNTS OF CHEMICAL RESEARCH

This journal publishes concise, critical reviews of research areas currently under active investigation. Most articles are written by scientists personally contributing to the area reviewed. Reviews need not be comprehensive. Indeed, they may be concerned in large part with work in the author's own laboratory.

Most reviews are written in response to invitations issued by the editor. First- and third-person nominations of prospective authors are welcomed; nominations should suggest the research area for review, and they should briefly summarize the prospective author's contributions to it. Unsolicited manuscripts are also considered for publication.

ACS SINGLE ARTICLE ANNOUNCEMENT

This is a semimonthly current awareness service based on 18 ACS journals and magazines. The announcement consists of the tables of contents from the latest issues of these journals, and a single copy of any item listed may be ordered.

ACS Symposium Series

This series is designed to publish symposia rapidly and economically. Papers are individually abstracted by *Chemical Abstracts* and undergo limited review.

Advances in Chemistry Series

This series of books provides an outlet for symposia that cannot be published in the Society's journals. The same rigorous standards of acceptance and editing that apply to material published in the journals also apply to material published in the *Advances*.

Decisions to publish symposia in this medium are made by the authors and the symposium chairman in collaboration with the series editor.

Analytical Chemistry

This research journal is devoted to all branches of analytical chemistry. Research papers are either theoretical with regard to analysis or are reports of laboratory experiments that support, argue, refute, or extend established theory. Research papers may contribute to any of the phases of analytical operations, such as sampling, preliminary chemical reactions, separations, instrumentation, measurements, and data processing. They need not necessarily refer to existing or even potential analytical methods in themselves but may be confined to the principles and methodology underlying such methods. Critical reviews of the literature, prepared by invitation, are published in April of each year in special issues which cover, in alternating years, applied and fundamental aspects of analysis.

Biochemistry

This journal publishes the results of original research that contribute significantly to biochemical knowledge. Preference will be accorded to manuscripts that generate new concepts or experimental approaches and are not merely depositories for scientific data. Hence, the primary criterion in the acceptance of manuscripts is that they present new or germinal findings or concepts.

CHEMICAL & ENGINEERING NEWS

As the official publication of the American Chemical Society and as a chemical newsweekly, C&EN is designed to keep ACS members informed of policies and activities of the ACS, to keep members as well as other readers well informed on the activities of the chemical world through news reporting and through calling attention to issues of consequence to chemists and chemical engineers, and to present the beneficial contributions of ACS and of its members to the broad goals of society at large.

CHEMICAL REVIEWS

Articles published in this journal are authoritative, critical, and comprehensive reviews of research in the various fields of chemistry. Preference is given to creative, timely reviews which will stimulate further research with a carefully selected subject and well-defined scope. In general, the topic should not have been reviewed in a readily available publication for about five years, though exceptions will be made if developments in the field have been particularly rapid, or if new insight can be achieved through further review of the subject.

Reviews are invited by the editor in response to suggestions from the editorial advisory board or elsewhere in the scientific community. Articles may also be accepted from authors who wish to contribute an unsolicited paper, provided that they contact the editor and obtain preliminary approval of the project, according to the procedure outlined in the "Suggestions to Authors" published in the journal.

CHEMISTRY

This magazine, appearing monthly except for two combined issues, January/February and July/August, is designed to appeal to students in the upper 40% of high school chemistry classes, to first-year college chemistry students, and to these students' teachers. It also has a wide appeal outside these groups as an interpreter of the science of chemistry. *Chemistry* presents and discusses basic chemical concepts and relates new developments within the discipline as well as those involving chemistry with other sciences and other human activities. Feature articles are usually written by a person active or even eminent in the field or by an able expositor of the subject. Some are staff-written. A Lab Bench section, presenting investigations readers can pursue in the laboratory, is usually included. Research reports are most often staff-written, though brief reports of findings written to interest beginning students are welcomed. Still briefer reports on chemistry and its influence are also carried. Readers' comments, questions and answers, and a Library-at-Large section are regularly included.

CHEMTECH

Every month *CHEMTECH* makes accessible a variety of useful tools for the mission-oriented chemist and engineer. Its concept orientation treats not only preparation, characterization, and uses of materials but also engineering design, operation, and distribution. Above all there is concern with the problems of the responsible technologist.

Each article is written by a recognized authority. Case history and workbook styles and multidisciplinary approach stimulate the broad-base awareness and interest that creative solutions to real problems require. Each issue treats the chemical technology of our vital needs—materials, energy, food, clothing, shelter, transport, medicine, and the like—as well as the interaction of individual sciences and technologies with each other and with socio-economic issues of the present and future.

ENVIRONMENTAL SCIENCE & TECHNOLOGY

This journal/magazine places special emphasis on reporting original chemical research, engineering developments, and technico-economic studies in fields of science directly related to man's environment. Contributed articles are directed to scientists and engineers concerned with fundamental and applied aspects of water, air, and waste chemistry. Because a meaningful approach to the management of environmental quality involves more than scientific understanding, the journal devotes serious attention to engineering, economic, legal, and other influences to give its readers an integrated view of this complex system. Contributed papers should describe results of original research. Review articles are considered when they serve to provide new research approaches or stimulate further worthwhile research in a significant area. The journal also publishes communications and a correspondence section.

INDUSTRIAL & ENGINEERING CHEMISTRY FUNDAMENTALS

Papers in the broad field of chemical engineering research are presented here. No technical field to which important contributions are being made is excluded—whether experimental or theoretical, mathematical or descriptive, chemical or physical. Acceptable papers are characterized by conclusions of some general significance, as distinguished from papers intended mainly to record data. Treatment of subjects is based on application of chemical, physical, and mathematical sciences, and papers are judged on their perceived lasting value.

INDUSTRIAL & ENGINEERING CHEMISTRY
PROCESS DESIGN AND DEVELOPMENT

Reports of original work on design methods and concepts and their application to the development of processes and process equipment are published in this journal. Empirical or semitheoretical correlations of data, experimental determinations of design parameters, methods of integrating systems analysis and process control into process design and development, scale-up procedures, and other experimental process development techniques are included.

INDUSTRIAL & ENGINEERING CHEMISTRY
PRODUCT RESEARCH AND DEVELOPMENT

Papers are published under the headings: Plenary Accounts, Technical Reviews, Product Reviews, Signals of Science, and General Articles. The last named section is (as papers are available) segmented under special headings such as Polymer, Catalyst, Coatings.

The function of the General Articles is to describe recent research results on the preparation, properties, and applications of chemicals and products derived therefrom. The review articles update the literature with an analytical assessment of current directions and recent new results. Signals of Science features the opportunity at an early period to expose novel findings which presage trend changes.

INORGANIC CHEMISTRY

This journal publishes original studies, both experimental and theoretical, in all phases of inorganic chemistry. These include synthesis and properties of new compounds, quantitative studies regarding structure, and thermodynamics and kinetics of inorganic reactions. In addition to notes, a correspondence section publishes short letters of scientific merit reporting results or scientific views. It provides a medium for the informal exchange of ideas but not preliminary communication of results.

JOURNAL OF AGRICULTURAL AND FOOD CHEMISTRY

This journal publishes research findings from the several interrelated chemical fields closely associated with the production, processing, and utilization of foods, feeds, fibers, and forestry products. Topics most frequently discussed are pesticides, fertilizers, plant growth regulators, the chemical composition of flavors, food materials, and other plant materials, the chemistry of nutrition, and the processing of food and farm needs. The papers submitted should report original research, and some practical significance should be apparent.

JOURNAL OF THE AMERICAN CHEMICAL SOCIETY

Original papers in all fields of chemistry are published here. Emphasis is placed on fundamental chemistry. Papers of general interest are sought, either because of their appeal to readers in more than one specialty or because they disclose findings of sufficient significance to command the interest of specialists in other fields. Communications and book reviews are also published. Specialized papers should be submitted to other journals of the Society.

JOURNAL OF CHEMICAL AND ENGINEERING DATA

This journal is directed to the publication of experimental or, in some cases, derived data in sufficient detail to form a working basis for applying the information to scientific or engineering objectives. Experimental methods should be referenced or described in enough detail to permit duplication of the data by others. The data should be presented with such precision that the results may be readily obtained within the stated limits of uncertainty of the experimental background. For most studies a tabular presentation or a mathematical description is preferred to the use of graphical methods.

JOURNAL OF CHEMICAL INFORMATION AND COMPUTER SCIENCES

The advancement of the knowledge, science, and art of chemical documentation is the aim of this journal. Papers published cover all aspects of chemical documentation, including information services and sources, technical writing, linguistics, indexing and classification systems and philosophies, correlation and communication of information, and description and evaluation of new tools, equipment, and machines.

JOURNAL OF MEDICINAL CHEMISTRY

This journal publishes articles, notes, and communications that contribute to an understanding of the relationship between molecular structure and biological activity. Some of the specific areas that are appropriate are: analysis of structure–activity relationships by a variety of approaches; design and synthesis of novel drugs; improvement of existing drugs by molecular modification; biochemical and pharmacological studies of receptor or enzyme mechanisms; isolation, structure elucidation, and synthesis of naturally occurring, biologically active molecules; new, improved syntheses of important drugs; physicochemical studies on established drugs which may furnish some insight into their mechanism of action; and the effect of molecular structure on the metabolism, distribution, and pharmacokinetics of drugs.

THE JOURNAL OF ORGANIC CHEMISTRY

The aim of this journal is to publish original and significant contributions in all branches of the theory and practice of organic chemistry. Areas emphasized include the many facets of organic reactions, natural products, bioorganic chemistry, studies of mechanism, theoretical organic chemistry, organometallic chemistry, and the various aspects of spectroscopy related to organic chemistry. This journal publishes articles, notes, and communications.

JOURNAL OF PHYSICAL AND CHEMICAL REFERENCE DATA

This journal is published quarterly by the American Chemical Society and the American Institute of Physics for the National Bureau of Standards. The objective of the journal is to provide critically evaluated physical and chemical property data, fully documented as to the original sources and the criteria used for evaluation. Critical reviews of measurement techniques, whose aim is to assess the accuracy of available data in a given technical area, are also included. The journal is not intended as a publication outlet for original experimental measurements such as are normally reported in the primary research literature, nor for review articles of a descriptive or primarily theoretical nature.

THE JOURNAL OF PHYSICAL CHEMISTRY

Original theoretical and experimental papers written for the specialist in physical chemistry are published in this journal. Preference is given to papers dealing with fundamental concepts, such as atomic and molecular phenomena or systems for which clearly defined models or definitions are forthcoming. Articles containing extensive reviews, reevaluations of existing data, and applied chemical data and papers dealing with measurements on materials of an ill-defined nature are, in general, not acceptable. Communications are also published.

MACROMOLECULES

This bimonthly journal publishes original research on all fundamental aspects of polymer chemistry, including synthesis, polymerization mechanisms and kinetics, chemical reactions, solution characteristics, and bulk properties of organic polymers, inorganic polymers, and biopolymers. The editors welcome regular articles, notes, communications, and occasional reviews.

II. THE SCIENTIFIC PAPER

Few of us understand everything we read at first reading. Even within one's own discipline, difficult concepts are not intuitively grasped. Clarity of expression, elegance of presentation, and simplicity of format are powerful means of enhancing understanding. The most convincing of scientific expositions will nevertheless be improved by a well-organized paper.

Rigid rules on manuscript preparation would be restrictive and counterproductive. Some journals of the Society are broad in scope; others are directed toward a single discipline. Books have special considerations. However, no field of science is completely independent of another, so most scientific papers, even in a journal of rigidly controlled scope, are multidisciplinary. The format of a paper devoted to mathematical exposition need not be the same as that of one discussing the determination of protein structure; both would be expected to differ from a study of synthetic methods or new process designs. A review would present different challenges and new problems. This handbook gives guidelines for preparing the traditional paper; the guidelines should be useful for the innovative and exceptional work as well. In addition, the handbook addresses the problem of a variety of composition systems, some with built-in restrictions and limitations, others with greater versatility and potential than previous approaches. Thus, the publication format and production method will dictate some elements of manuscript preparation.

Before a paper is written, the following questions should be answered: What journal would be the most appropriate outlet for the publication? What types of papers does that journal publish? Into which of those categories would this work best fit?

The major types of presentation in the journals of the American Chemical Society are articles, notes, communications, and reviews. Not all journals contain all of these, and some use other forms. Lists of the categories possible and a brief discussion of each are contained in the instructions to authors of each of the journals. (*See* the first issue of each volume.)

ARTICLES (published in all the books and journals except *Accounts of Chemical Research* and *Chemical Reviews,* which publish reviews exclusively)

These are definitive accounts of significant, completed studies. They should present important new data or provide a fresh approach to an established subject.

The organization and length of these contributions are determined largely by the data to be presented and are governed by space restrictions within the publication. The traditional mode of presentation is suitable for most papers in this category. Many papers contain material that would be suitable for a supplementary type of publication outlet (for a discussion of this approach, *see* Microform Supplements in Section III).

NOTES (published in *Environmental Science & Technology, Inorganic Chemistry, Journal of Medicinal Chemistry, The Journal of Organic Chemistry,* and *Macromolecules*)

These contributions are concise accounts of studies of a limited scope. The material reported must be definitive and may not be republished elsewhere. Improved procedures of wide applicability or interest, accounts of novel observations or of compounds of special interest, and development of a technique often constitute useful notes. Notes are distinguished formally from articles in some journals by the absence of a printed abstract, but they are subjected to the same editorial appraisal as full-length articles.

COMMUNICATIONS (published in *Industrial & Engineering Chemistry Fundamentals, Industrial & Engineering Chemistry Process Design and Development, Journal of Agricultural and Food Chemistry, Journal of the American Chemical Society, Journal of Medicinal Chemistry, The Journal of Organic Chemistry, The Journal of Physical Chemistry,* and *Macromolecules*)

These are preliminary reports of special significance and urgency that are given expedited publication. They will be accepted if in the opinion of the editors their rapid publication will be of real service to the scientific community. They should not exceed 1000 words, yet they must contain specific results to support their conclusions. Polemics should be avoided and nonessential experimental details should be omitted.

Communications are submitted to review, and they are not accepted if in the opinion of the editor the principal content has been published or publicized elsewhere. The same rigorous standards of acceptance that apply to full-length articles also apply to communications. These contributions differ from articles and notes in that the authors are expected to publish complete details, not necessarily in the same journal, after their communications have appeared. Acceptance of a communication, however, does not guarantee acceptance of the detailed manuscript.

REVIEWS (published in *Accounts of Chemical Research, Analytical Chemistry, Chemical Reviews, CHEMTECH, Environmental Science & Technology, Industrial & Engineering Chemistry Fundamentals, Industrial & Engineering Chemistry Process Design and Development, Industrial & Engineering Chemistry Product Research and Development, Macromolecules,* symposium books, and other journals if editorial judgment so advises)

Reviews integrate and correlate results from numerous articles and notes which are relevant to the subject under review. They seldom report new experimental findings. Effective review articles have a well-defined theme, are usually critical, and may present novel theoretical interpretations. Ordinarily they do not give experimental details, but in special cases (as when a technique is of central interest) experimental procedures may be included. An important function of reviews is to serve as a guide to the original literature; for this reason adequacy of bibliographical citation is essential.

The character and scope of reviews vary considerably from journal to journal. For example, in *Accounts of Chemical Research* the focus is often on recent developments in the laboratory of the author or on the critical examination of a controversial topic; in *Chemical Reviews,* a broader topic is pursued in depth. Earlier statements concerning individual American Chemical Society journals indicate the type of review each publishes (Section I).

MISCELLANEOUS

In addition to these types of presentation, the following forms are worth noting:

"Correspondence" in *Analytical Chemistry* consists of brief disclosures of special significance, reports of work which the authors do not plan to continue, or exchanges of view among authors.

"Correspondence" in *Environmental Science & Technology, Industrial & Engineering Chemistry Fundamentals, Industrial & Engineering Chemistry Process Design and Development,* and *Industrial & Engineering Chemistry Product Research and Development* consists of short contributions relating to previously published articles and presenting either alternative interpretations or additional data of interest. These contributions are reviewed by the author of the original publication, who is given the opportunity to publish simultaneous correspondence if he wishes.

"Correspondence" in *Inorganic Chemistry* consists of short letters reporting results or scientific views.

"Aids" in *Analytical Chemistry* are brief descriptions of novel apparatus or techniques.

"Data Compilations" in *Journal of Chemical and Engineering Data* are brief reviews by the editorial staff of secondary publications on data compilations.

"New Compounds" in *Journal of Chemical and Engineering Data* are brief descriptions of syntheses and properties of well-defined compounds, both organic and inorganic, of potential scientific and technological interest and importance in all physical and biological areas where current data are not available. Guidelines for authors are available from the editor.

"Experimental Techniques" in *Industrial & Engineering Chemistry Fundamentals* include descriptions of novel apparatus, instruments, procedures, or methods of laboratory observation and measurement designed for laboratory research. Experimental results or theoretical interpretation are accepted only to support the experimental method itself. Descriptions of commercial instruments are not suitable, and discussions of well-known procedures are included only if they make substantial contributions to new, inventive uses of the older methods.

Organization

Logical organization of the material to be presented is of key importance. Thoughtful consideration of the subject and anticipation of the reader's needs and questions will usually indicate to the writer the type of organization required. Although variations from conventional form are permitted, certain elements are considered standard parts of the manuscript. The following suggestions are intended primarily for full-length articles but are applicable to notes and communications with some modification.

When several closely related manuscripts are being prepared at about the same time, they should be submitted simultaneously. This permits editors and reviewers to examine the manuscripts in an overall context and reduces the possibility of fragmentation of the work.

INTRODUCTORY MATERIAL

Title. The title of a technical document should tell accurately and clearly what the document is about. Choose title terms that are as specific as the content and emphasis of the paper permit; for example, "a vanadium–iron alloy" would be better than "a magnetic alloy". Balance brevity against descriptive accuracy and completeness. A two- or three-word title may be too cryptic. On the other hand a 14- or 15-word title is probably unnecessarily long. Ideally, a title should be an ultrabrief abstract. An article entitled "Metallurgical Analysis" is ambiguous. "Simultaneous Spectrophotometric Determination of Iron and Chromium in Steel" would be more descriptive. Avoid unnecessary phrases ("on the," "a study of") and articles (a, an, the).

A high keyword content is generally valuable to attract the potential audience of a paper and to aid retrieval and indexing services. A series title is of little value. (Consecutive papers in a series, published simultaneously, are generally sufficiently closely related so that a series title may be relevant, but paper 42 probably bears sufficiently little relationship in methodology or on subject to paper 1 as to be an unwarranted parallelism; in addition, the editor or reviewer may be prejudiced against the paper—one more publication on a general topic that has already been discussed at length.)

Symbols, formulas, and abbreviations should be avoided in titles. It is preferable to spell out each term. Whenever possible use words rather than expressions containing superscripts, subscripts, or other special notations, in order to facilitate machine indexing and retrieval.

Byline and Affiliation Information. Every manuscript should have a byline containing the names of all those who have made substantial contributions to the work being reported: first names, initials, and surnames should be included. (First initials, second names, and surnames are equally acceptable. Use of initials and surname is not recommended—it causes indexing and·retrieval difficulties and interferes with unique identification of an author.) Consistency in using names is also recommended (papers by J. Smith, J. R. Smith, John R. Smith, J. Smith, Jr., J. R. Smith, Jr., and John R. Smith, Jr., will not be indexed at one spot; the bibliographic citations may be scattered at six points, and ascribing the work to a single author will therefore be difficult.) In some journals the name(s) of the institution and the city in which the study was conducted are also included. In other journals this information is given as a footnote to the title.

Even if the manuscript itself has been written by one person, the names of those who have contributed essential portions of the work are usually listed as authors. The author to whom correspondence and reprint requests should be addressed is indicated by an asterisk. If the present affiliation of the author to whom correspondence should be directed is different from that held when the work was done, the new address should be given in a footnote. New addresses for coauthors are not, however, published in all of the journals.

Many secondary services restrict the number of author index entries associated with each paper. In *Chemical Abstracts,* the maximum number of index entries is 10. Thus, with 11 or more authors, the first 9 and et al. will be used in the abstracts, issue index, volume index, and data base.

Abstract. Except for reviews in journals and for *ACS Symposium Series,* every paper must be accompanied by an informative abstract that summarizes the principal findings of the work reported in the paper. Although usually read first, the abstract should be written last to ensure that it reflects accurately the content of the paper.

Through a cooperative effort between the primary and secondary publications of the American Chemical Society, a drastic reduction in the time lag between journal publication and abstract publication in *Chemical Abstracts* is taking place. This is being accomplished through the direct use by *Chemical Abstracts* of the abstracts submitted with the original papers. In most cases, the abstract is being processed for publication in *Chemical Abstracts* at the same time that the manuscript is in press.

For this effort to achieve maximum success, it is essential that the author be aware of the importance given to the abstract. The ideal abstract will briefly state the problem, or the purpose of the research when that information is not adequately contained in the title, indicate the theoretical or experimental plan used, accurately summarize the principal findings, and point out major conclusions. The author should keep in mind the purpose of the abtract, which is to allow the reader to determine what kind of information is in a given paper and to pinpoint key features for use in indexing and eventual retrieval. The abstract is not intended as a substitute for the article itself, but it must contain sufficient information to allow a reader to ascertain his interest in the subject. The abstract should provide adequate data for the generation of index entries concerning the kind of information present and key compounds. (Issue indexes for *Chemical Abstracts* are generated from titles and abstracts of papers. Volume indexes of most ACS journals are generated from the *CA* issue indexes. However, the volume indexes for *Chemical Abstracts* itself are based upon the complete document being indexed.) Chemical safety information, when applicable, should also be noted.

The abstract should be concise (the optimum length could be two sentences; it could be many more, depending upon subject matter and length of paper), self-contained, and representative of the technical content of the document. (Abstracts for *Advances in Chemistry Series* books are limited to 125 words or less.) The nomenclature used should be meaningful; that is, standard systematic nomenclature should be used where specificity and complexity require or "trivial" nomenclature where this will adequately and unambiguously define a well-established compound. Tables and figures should not be cited or included. References to equations or structures presented in the body of the paper may be made in the abstract because these may readily be incorporated when the abstract is used in *Chemical Abstracts* (*see* Figures 1 and 2). Equations and structures that are not linear and cannot be incorporated in the text should be avoided. Symbols such as $\rightarrow$ should not be used because material set over and under arrows creates composition difficulties. Abbreviations should be used sparingly, and only when necessary to prevent awkward construction or needless repetition. Abbreviations not listed on pp 38–42 should be defined at first use.

Although abstracts are not printed for some categories of material, they are still essential for the secondary services. In the interest of more rapid publication and since the author should be the best judge of what

The flash photolysis resonance fluorescence technique was employed to investigate the temperature dependencies of the reactions $Cl + CH_4 \rightarrow HCl + CH_3$ (k_1); $Cl + CH_3Cl \rightarrow HCl + CH_2Cl$ (k_2); $Cl + CH_3F \rightarrow HCl + CH_2F$ (k_3); $Cl + CH_3F^\dagger \rightarrow HCl + CH_2F$ (k_3'); $Cl + C_2H_6 \rightarrow HCl + C_2H_5$ (k_4). The following rate expressions were obtained in units of cm^3 molecule^{-1} s^{-1}: k_1(218–322 K) = (7.93 ± 1.53) × 10^{-12} exp[−(2529 ± 101)/RT]; k_2(233–322 K) = (3.36 ± 0.71) × 10^{-11} exp[−(2484 ± 113)/RT]; k_3(216–296 K) = (4.79 ± 1.05) × 10^{-12} exp[−(1535 ± 107)/RT]; k_4(222–322 K) = (7.29 ± 1.23) × 10^{-11} exp[−(121 ± 87)/RT] where R = 1.987 cal deg^{-1} mol^{-1}. At 227 and 296 K k_3'/k_3 was observed to be ≤1.3.

ABSTRACT: The envelope glycoproteins (designated gp70 and gp45) of the Rauscher strain of murine leukemia virus were solubilized by osmotic shock and freeze-thawing in chaotropic solutions. The viral glycoproteins were then purified by phosphocellulose chromatography and gel permeation chromatography on Bio-Gel A-1.5m. Yields by this procedure were 6.2% for gp70 and 1.3% for gp45 on a protein input basis. The apparent molecular weights were respectively 67 500 and 47 500 with a polypeptide chain molecular weight of approximately 45 000 for both glycoproteins. Amino acid analysis showed a high degree of similarity for both components, with some differences subject to further evaluation. The total carbohydrate content was approximately 32% for gp70 and 6–9% for gp45. In keeping with the amino acid compositional similarity suggesting relationships, alanine was found to be the amino-terminal amino acid of both glycoproteins, and cross-reactivity was demonstrated by immunologic tests. The data suggest that the chief difference between gp70 and gp45 lies in the carbohydrate content.

Figure 1. Typical abstracts from *The Journal of Physical Chemistry* (top) and *Biochemistry* (bottom).

3,3-Diphenyl-1-nitrocyclohexene was synthesized for photochemical study in order to compare nitro n–π* photochemistry with carbonyl n–π* reactivity. Both direct and sensitized irradiations in benzene gave rise to *trans*-5,6-diphenyl-1-nitrobicyclo[3.1.0]hexane; the preference for formation of trans product was shown to be kinetic. Additionally, the photolysis afforded 3,3-diphenylcyclohexanone. Quantum efficiencies were determined, and these were found to be quite low compared with the corresponding enone analogue. Thus, for formation of bicyclic nitro compound the unsensitized and sensitized efficiencies were found to be $\phi = 3.05 \times 10^{-4}$ and 4.52×10^{-4} (acetophenone). Evidence favoring triplet multiplicity of the rearranging species is discussed as is the low reaction efficiency. It was observed that irradiation in isopropyl alcohol gave rise to 3,3-diphenylcyclohexanone oxime as the major product with the oxime to bicyclic product ratio increasing with increasing isopropyl alcohol concentration in isopropyl alcohol–benzene mixtures. Finally, *cis*-5,6-diphenyl-1-nitrobicyclo[3.1.0]hexane was independently synthesized by reaction of 2-phenyl-1-nitrocyclopentene with diphenylsulfonium benzylide. This stereoisomer was converted, both in direct and sensitized irradiations, to the trans stereoisomer with a steady state favoring trans isomer over 1000:1.

86: 88870t **Photochemical rearrangements of an unsaturated nitro compound. Mechanistic and exploratory organic photochemistry.** 103. Zimmerman, Howard E.; Roberts, Luther C.; Arnold, Roberta (Dep. Chem., Univ. Wisconsin, Madison, Wis.). *J. Org. Chem.* 1977, 42(4), 621–9 (Eng).

Both direct and sensitized irradn. of 3,3-diphenyl-1-nitrocyclohexane (**I**) gave *trans*-5,6-diphenyl-1-nitrobicyclo[3.1.0]hexane (**II**) by kinetic control. Addnl., the photolysis afforded 3,3-diphenylcyclohexanone. Quantum efficiencies were low compared with the corresponding enone analog. Evidence favoring triplet multiplicity of the rearranging species is discussed. Irradn. of **I** in Me₂CHOH gave 3,3-diphenylcyclohexanone oxime as the major product with the oxime to bicyclic product ratio increasing with increasing alc. in Me₂CHOH–C₆H₆ mixts. Also, *cis*-5,6-diphenyl-1-nitrobicyclo[3.1.0]hexane was converted, both in direct and sensitized irradns., to the trans stereoisomer with a steady state favoring trans isomer 1000:1.

Figure 2. Comparison of abstracts in the primary journal (top, *The Journal of Organic Chemistry*) and the secondary publication (bottom, *Chemical Abstracts*). Note the inclusion of structures in the latter.

the abstract should contain, all manuscripts (except those mentioned above) must be accompanied by an abstract that meets the preceding requirements. It will be processed by *Chemical Abstracts* simultaneously with its companion material.

For a more detailed guide to the preparation of abstracts, consult "American National Standard for Writing Abstracts" (*see* Bibliography).

THE REPORT

Authors have a higher probability of their papers' being understood and accepted for publication if the papers meet certain standards in originality, style, and organization.

Originality: the paper should make a contribution. It should be written with an awareness of the primary and secondary audiences and of the specific journal or book involved. Duplicate publication is not permissible, and fragmented publication should be avoided.

Style: the author should be logical, clear, direct, concise. Papers should be directed to the specialist, but they should not use, without definition, terminology that is intelligible only to the specialist.

Organization: the primary aim is to facilitate communication. There is no ideal format to follow. What would be suitable for one topic could be unworkable with another. Therefore, the sections discussed below are only guidelines; they are applicable to most papers.

Although the different parts of the main body of the report need not be labeled as such and do not need to be in the sequence suggested here, they should include an introduction, an experimental section (e.g., materials and methods) when pertinent, results, and a discussion.

The journals differ in their preferences for headings. It is generally redundant to label the initial section "introduction". Theoretical reports may have a mathematical instead of an experimental section, or the equivalent of the latter may not occur at all.

Introduction. A good introduction states the problem clearly; it gives the background of the work and the approach used by the author. Here the author should give the significance of the work in the context of what is known, should orient the reader to the problem, and should outline what has been done before by citing truly pertinent literature. A general survey of semirelevant literature should *not* be included.

Experimental Section. Enough detail should be given in this section so that other experienced workers familiar with the field could repeat the work and obtain comparable results.

(1) Materials used must be identified. Information on the degree of and criteria for purity should be included. Reagents normally available in the laboratory should not be referenced.

(2) Apparatus should be described *only if not standard,* with a drawing in specialized cases, and with names of specific equipment and source, if not well-known. Commercially available instruments should not be described.

(3) Procedures should be described. For experiments involving established procedures, references and characterization of the products [*see* (1) above] may suffice.

Any unexpected hazards encountered with the experimental work must be noted and emphasized. (This should generally be in a separate paragraph, introduced by the word **Caution.**)

The accuracy of primary measurements must be stated. Theoretical reports should contain sufficient mathematical detail to enable derivations to be reproduced and numerical results to be checked. Also, all background data, equations, and formulas necessary to the argument should be included in this section of the manuscript. Formulas of compounds, except those of common substances, should be given at least once, together with the appropriate chemical name.

In some papers, the experimental section is the most important part of the presentation. In others, it is secondary. In addition, there are often large segments of information that would be of interest to the specialist attempting to duplicate the results but would be of little value to the general reader. To serve the combined mutual interests of journal space, author value, and reader need, microfiche or "miniprint" publication alternatives are occasionally desirable (*see* section on Microform Supplements and Miniprint Material).

Results and Discussion. For most papers the presentation of results and discussion of their significance may be separated into two distinct sections. Occasionally, however, a chronological approach may be preferable (e.g., theoretical considerations followed by a set of experiments and a discussion of results that leads to a second set of experiments). Regardless of the outline followed by the author, the following points should be noted:

(1) Only relevant data should be included. Equations, figures, and tables should be used where necessary for *clarity and conciseness*. In general the same data should not be reported in both figures and tables.

(2) Numerical data should be reported in SI units (*see* Section III and Appendix A), and dimensions, when applicable, must be included.

(3) In the discussion of the significance of the results, an objective explanation is essential. The features and limitations of the work should be pointed out, and the results should be interpreted, compared, and contrasted.

(4) A summary may add to the value of the presentation. It should be interpretive and not repetitious. The problem may not have been completely solved; if so, further study may be suggested.

Acknowledgments. Contributions of persons, other than coauthors, who have added substantially to the work may be acknowledged in a separate paragraph at the end of the paper. Supporting staff including draftsmen, machinists, and secretaries should not ordinarily be mentioned. Recognition of assistance should be stated as simply as possible.

Nontechnical information such as grant numbers and sponsors also should be included in this paragraph, in a separate terminal paragraph, or in a footnote, as should mention of preliminary presentation of the material at a meeting. (Consult the instructions to authors of each journal for specific instructions.) In books, grant numbers and sponsors are listed after the "Received" line.

References. Most journals and the symposium books publish references at the end of the paper; a few treat them as footnotes (*see* p 72 ff). An attempt has been made to standardize as much as possible the format and content of references regardless of where they are located.

Special Sections. The preceding discussion applies to most manuscripts, but it is not meant to exclude any portion of a paper that does not fall under the headings given. For example: many papers have glossary and notation sections; appendixes can form an important part of a paper; the use of the supplementary material program is expanding (*see* Microform Supplements); biographical sketches are an integral part of many review articles. Thus, a paper need not conform to a series of rigid rules and headings so long as it is well organized and scientifically sound, novel, and appropriate to the mission of the publication to which it is submitted.

III. THE MANUSCRIPT

The readability of any paper is enhanced by consistency of format and style. This section presents details of manuscript preparation. Topics that are discussed include preferred spellings and punctuation usages, handling of words and numbers, conventions for abbreviations and symbols, nomenclature, preparation of tables and illustrations, format for documentation, requirements for submission of final copy (including some of the limitations inherent in the composition technique involved; *see* Appendix E), and discussion of alternative publication formats and future manuscript requirements.

The recommendations that follow are presented not to restrict unnecessarily the author's individuality but to provide general guidelines that will help in presentation. Manuscripts prepared and submitted according to editorial requirements can be reviewed and processed for publication more efficiently and rapidly.

The notes on style included here are not intended to be a complete treatment of the subject. They merely point out some of the recurring problems troublesome to editors and authors. Most of the following suggestions apply to all books and journals. In a few instances tradition has led to a somewhat different style for some aspects of manuscripts; this handbook attempts to point out these variations wherever they occur. Authors should also consult the instructions to authors and current copies of the publication to which they will submit their manuscript to familiarize themselves with format, conventions, and details of style for that journal or book, after which they should settle upon a consistent style for their manuscript.

Style

SPELLING

Use American spelling rather than British, except in names and direct quotations. When in doubt, consult a dictionary. Webster's "New World

Dictionary of the American Language", Second College Edition, is preferred. Webster's "New International Dictionary", Third Edition, will continue to be used as an auxiliary reference. In a few instances more than one spelling is commonly accepted for the same word; the author should choose one spelling and use it consistently throughout his paper. A list of preferred spellings for words and expressions often encountered in the books and journals is included in Appendix C.

For accepted chemical terminology, the references on nomenclature given on p 115 are valuable. In addition, the "Condensed Chemical Dictionary", the "Merck Index", "The SOCMA (Synthetic Organic Chemical Manufacturers Association) Handbook of Commercial Organic Chemical Names",* "The U.S. Pharmacopeia", and "USAN" (United States Adopted Names) are also recommended. The "Technical Speller" and, for the spelling of trademarks, the "thomas Register of American Manufacturers" may also be useful (*see* pp 114–117).

Hyphens. Good usage sometimes sanctions more than one form in combining the elements of a compound word (two or more terms used to express a single idea). It is difficult to prescribe, for all circumstances, when to use a hyphen, when to write one word, and when to write separate words. Hyphens must be used when necessary to ensure correct interpretation of intended meaning. For compound words in common usage, follow the form used in Webster's. Several examples are also included in the preferred spelling list (Appendix C). A few general rules are given here as guides:

(1) A compound word functioning as an adjective and placed before the noun it modifies is usually hyphenated. However, when the modifier contains three terms, the hyphenation is arbitrary, but should be between all or none.

a melting-point determination (a determination of melting point)
a low-molecular-weight compound or a low molecular weight compound (a compound of low molecular weight)

(2) The names of chemical compounds that are unhyphenated when used as nouns remain unhyphenated when used as adjectives. Exceptions are made if required by specific nomenclature recommendations (e.g., the glucose 6-phosphate pathway; but, in enzyme nomenclature, glucose-6-phosphate isomerase).

a sodium chloride solution
a barium sulfate precipitate

---

* Out of print, but still an excellent reference.

Note: A solidus or a dash, not a hyphen, is used between components of a mixed solvent.

The melting point was unchanged after three crystallizations from hexane/benzene (or hexane–benzene).

(3) Hyphens are used to set apart numbers, Greek letters, configurational letters, and italicized prefixes in chemical names.

2-benzoylbenzoic acid, cholesterol 3β-acetate
D-arabinose, *trans*-2-bromocyclopentanol

(4) Do not hyphenate adverb–adjective combinations.

accurately measured values
a carefully planned experiment

(5) When two or more unit modifiers have the same base, use a hyphen after each element dependent upon that base.

25-, 50-, and 100-mL flasks

(6) The following prefixes usually are not hyphenated: after, anti, auto, co, de, down, electro, infra, iso, metallo, mid, macro, micro, non, over, pre, photo, physico, poly, post, re, semi, sub, stereo, up, un, ultra, visco.

PUNCTUATION

The importance of correct punctuation cannot be overemphasized. Misplaced commas·can distort meaning, and missing marks may detract from easy comprehension. In addition, computer technology for automatic abstracting, indexing, and editing will not be effective unless the material analyzed is properly punctuated. (*See J. Chem. Inf. Comput. Sci.* **1975**, *15,* 226, for a discussion of automatic abstracting.)

For general rules of punctuation the author may wish to consult a handbook of English composition or a dictionary. The Books Department uses "A Manual of Style", University of Chicago Press, as authority for grammar and punctuation. However, punctuation to be used in footnotes, references, abbreviations, and chemical and mathematical expressions should follow the usage recommended in the corresponding sections of this handbook. The following suggestions should be especially noted:

(1) Do not use a period after symbols and most abbreviations.

(2) Punctuate all simple series (three or more entries) with commas.

(3) Place a comma before "and" and "or" in a simple series.

(4) Do not use commas in writing numbers of four or more digits. A period is used for the decimal sign.

(5) Use a comma after an introductory clause unless the clause is extremely short.

(6) Use a comma to separate the independent clauses in compound sentences unless the clauses are short and closely related.

(7) Use a colon to separate parts of ratios.

(8) Use the sequence ([( )]) for signs of aggregation in chemical and mathematical expressions except where conventional notation specifies some other order. However, [(( ))] and [[( )]] are acceptable combinations.

(9) In manuscripts the dash should be typed as two hyphens: --.

(10) Quotation marks are used to enclose only material being quoted, or for emphasis. [When quotations are used in this handbook, the closing mark follows journal practice; books use the style recommended by the Chicago Manual.]

HANDLING OF WORDS

Numerous authoritative texts on rhetoric, style, and grammar are available. A list of valuable source books is included in this handbook. Authors may find the recommended references to language and technical writing helpful as detailed guides to correct usage (*see* pp 114–117).

In writing a report the author should strive for conciseness and clarity. Words and expressions should be chosen carefully to convey the correct meaning.

(1) Do not introduce sentences by "it was found that" or "it was demonstrated that".

(2) Where directness is desired, use the active voice. Avoid passive constructions. Do not use first person plural when singular is appropriate.

(3) Avoid unnecessary words; logic prohibits such duplication as:

estimated at *about* 10%
such as copper, iron, *etc.*
bright red *in color*
fewer *in number*
oval *in shape*
they are *both* alike
throughout the *entire* experiment
two *equal* halves

Wordy expressions may often be substituted by a simple word. For example:

owing to the fact that—because
subsequent to—after
on the order of—about
in the near future—soon
at the present time—now
by means of—by
it appears that—apparently
of great importance—important
in consequence of this fact—therefore
a very limited number of—few

Two of the most common punctuation errors occur with the words whereas and however. A "whereas" clause is never independent. Typical misuse:

The activity on bromopyruvate was decreased; whereas, the activity on pyruvate was enhanced.

The activity on bromopyruvate was decreased, however the activity on pyruvate was enhanced.

The correct punctuation is indicated in the margin.

In general, authors should use generic terminology rather than specific commercial identification. For example, substitute petroleum jelly for Vaseline, camera for Kodak, silicon carbide for Carborundum, fiber insulation board for Celotex, photocopy for Xerox.

Manuscripts should be free of grammatical errors. Certain faulty constructions or stylistic flaws are likely to be confusing. A list of terms commonly misused by writers and examples of constructions that offer special hazards are included in Appendix D.

SPECIAL TYPE (ITALICS, BOLDFACE, SMALL CAPS)

Special type helps the reader quickly distinguish letters, words, or phrases from the rest of the text. All material that is to appear in *italics* when printed is underscored by a simple straight line in the manuscript. Entries requiring **boldface** type are marked with a wavy underline. SMALL CAPITALS are indicated by underlining twice.

Recommendations and specific examples regarding the conventional use of special type faces for abbreviations and symbols, in references, and in footnotes are included in the sections of the handbook pertinent to these subjects. Authors must pay particular attention to the required use of italics in nomenclature and for symbols but should not mark the manuscript for special type to avoid requesting possibly incorrect, and thus misleading, marks.

The following rules should be noted:

(1) Italics should be used sparingly to emphasize a word or phrase; long passages should not be italicized.

(2) Foreign words and phrases (except journal titles) and Latin expressions and abbreviations, such as ca., vs., et al., etc., i.e., e.g., in common use in English writing should not be italicized.

(3) Chemical formulas are not italicized. Hyphenated prefixes to formulas and in names, such as cis-, trans-, o-, m-, p-, however, should be underlined for italics in the manuscript; thus, *cis-*, *trans-*, *o-*, *m-*, *p-*. When used alone, these prefixes are not italic (cis isomer, for example). However, the configurational prefixes R, S, E, and Z should always be italic, as should d and l (rotation).

(4) Greek letters and trigonometric terms such as sin, tan, cos, log, mod should not be underlined in the manuscript.

(5) The scientific names of genera and species are italicized.

(6) Names of periodicals and their abbreviations are italicized.

NUMBERS AND MATHEMATICAL EXPRESSIONS

To prevent errors by the printer, subscripts, superscripts, Greek letters, and other symbols should be clearly identified (by a note in the margin if necessary). In particular, a clear distinction should be made between the following: (a) capital and lower case letters when used as symbols; (b) zero and the letter "o"; (c) the small letter "el", the numeral one, and a prime sign; (d) the letters "k" and κ (kappa), "u" and μ (mu), "v" and ν (nu), "n" and η (eta).

Care should be observed in using the solidus (slant) and brackets to avoid ambiguities in equations.

The following rules represent accepted practice in writing numbers:

(1) Use figures with units of measurement.

samples of 0.30 and 0.16 g
a 25-μL aliquot
yields of 63–65%
a factor of 3

(2) Use figures for all cardinal numbers 10 and above unless they are used to start a sentence.

and 12 test tubes

(3) Use figures for all ordinal numbers greater than 10 (11th, 23rd). Ordinal numbers less than 11 (third, tenth) may be spelled out. However, within one sentence only one form is permitted.

the 11th and 12th lines
the 2nd and 20th samples
the first and third equations

(4) Use decimals rather than fractions for mixed numbers, unless doing so would imply a nonexisting accuracy.

2.5 s (not 2½ s); 5.25 g (not 5¼ g); 2⅔ (acceptable; not 2.67)

(5) Spell out numbers at the beginning of a sentence, or preferably recast the sentence to avoid putting numbers first. (In figure captions, this practice may be ignored.)

Twenty slides were examined
Fifty grams was treated
A 50-g sample was added

(6) Do not repeat the same number in both numerals and words; for example, do not write "a sequence of five (5) measurements".

(7) Place a zero before the decimal point in writing numbers with no integer.

0.50   0.175

(8) In numbers with five or more digits preceding or following the decimal sign, separate the digits by a space into groups of three, counting from the decimal sign toward the left or right. In numbers with four digits, the space is not necessary. (This practice facilitates the reading of numbers and eliminates confusion from differing uses of the comma and period in various parts of the world. However, in equations all numbers should be written without spaces: $32425x + ...$)

12 531   7465   9.2163   0.102 834

(9) In tables, to facilitate reading numbers, spaces *should* be used with four-digit numbers in columns containing numbers of five or more digits preceding or following the decimal point (first example of column one). Alternatively, if there are only a few numbers of five or more digits, it is not necessary to use a space (last example in column three; contrary to point 8, but acceptable).

0.812 5	3 251 651	0.8182
12.856 78	3 259 509	0.5749
1022.752 97	3 254 072	0.00483

(10) Use of an exponential number is encouraged where it will save space.

3.2×10^6 rather than   3 200 000

(11) Within the framework of the SI system of units, numbers larger than four digits can be avoided by choosing an appropriate multiplicative prefix for the unit.

(12) Attention should be given to include no more than the appropriate number of significant figures.

(13) When exponential powers of 10 are used in designating the coordinates of graphs or column heads in tables, the exponential power of 10 should apply to the numerical value in the quantity, not to the unit. For example, the labels could read wavelength $\times 10^{-3}$/nm for axes of 1, 2, 3, etc., or for column heads with column data of 1, 2, 3, etc., when the wavelengths represented are 1000 nm, 2000 nm, 3000 nm, etc.

(14) Numbers and mathematical expressions are subject to various rules and conventions for spacing and typesetting. Write:

$(3.24 \pm 0.01)10^{12}$
$20 \pm 2\%$
25 g ($\pm 1\%$)   (not $25 \pm 1\%$ g)

(15) Multiplication and division may be indicated in the following ways:

a multiplied by b	ab
a divided by b	a/b, ab^{-1}

$\dfrac{a}{b}$ in display equations only, when it is not feasible to use a linear expression

When the quantities being multiplied or divided are themselves products, quotients, sums, or differences of other quantities, parentheses must be used in accordance with the rules of mathematics. If the solidus (/) is used in division and if there is any doubt where the numerator starts or where the denominator ends, parentheses should be used. More than one solidus should never be used in the same expression unless parentheses are inserted to eliminate ambiguity.

$(a/b)/c$ or $a/(b/c)$; never $a/b/c$

It is recommended that in expressions such as

$\sin [2\pi(x - x_0)/\lambda]$, $\exp[-V(r)/kT]$,

the argument should always be placed within brackets, except when the argument is a simple product of two quantities:

$$\sin kx$$

(16) Preferred style for mathematical expressions varies as follows (the technical editor will underline for italic type)

for expressions in text or in display equations	for expressions in display equations
a/(bcd)	$\dfrac{a}{bcd}$
(2/9) sin kx, $\frac{2}{9}$ sin kx	$\dfrac{2}{9} \sin kx$
(1/2)RT, $\frac{1}{2}$RT, RT/2	$\dfrac{1}{2}$RT, $\dfrac{RT}{2}$
(a/b) − c	$\dfrac{a}{b} - c$
a/(b − c)	$\dfrac{a}{b-c}$
(a − b)/(c − d)	$\dfrac{a-b}{c-d}$
(a/c) − (b/d)	$\dfrac{a}{c} - \dfrac{b}{d}$

(17) Roman numerals should be used selectively; numbers greater than X should be avoided.

(18) A few examples of usages and symbols for mathematical operations and constants as they should appear in the manuscript are listed below.

approximately equal to	$\approx$
asymptotically equal to	$\sim$
proportional to	$\propto$
approaches (tends to)	$\rightarrow$
absolute magnitude of a	$|a|$
identical with	$\equiv$
square root of a	$\sqrt{a}$, $a^{1/2}$
nth root of a	$\sqrt[n]{a}$, $a^{1/n}$
mean value of a	$\bar{a}$, $\langle a \rangle$
logarithm to the base 10 of x	log x
logarithm to the base a of x	$\log_a$ x
natural logarithm of x	ln x
finite increment of x	Δx
infinitesimal increment of x	∂x

total differential of x	dx
function of x	$f(x)$
integral of y with respect to x	$\int y\,dx$
integral of y from $x = a$ to $x = b$	$\int_a^b y\,dx$
vector of magnitude A	$\underset{\sim}{A}$
scalar product of **A** and **B**	$\underset{\sim}{A} \cdot \underset{\sim}{B}$
vector product of **A** and **B**	$\underset{\sim}{A} \times \underset{\sim}{B},\ \underset{\sim}{A}\underset{\sim}{B}$
matrix A	$\underset{\sim}{\underset{\sim}{A}}$

Abbreviations, Symbols, and Units

Abbreviations hinder comprehension by readers in fields other than that of the author, by abstractors, and by scientists in other countries. Therefore, it is the policy of American Chemical Society books and journals to reduce use of abbreviations to a minimum.

Before an author decides to use an abbreviation, he should consider the following points: (a) Is the use warranted? Only repeated citation of a long term is reason for shortening that term. (b) Is the abbreviation common enough to be immediately intelligible to most readers? (These are the only type permitted in titles. NMR, DNA, and RNA are among the few abbreviations in this category. Other abbreviations should not be used in titles. In addition, with the exception of the symbols for the chemical elements and the amino acids, most abbreviations should be adequately identified in the abstract and defined, according to journal practice, in the paper itself.) (c) Is there a recommended form for the abbreviation? If not, it should be formulated according to established practice in the field.

A specialized abbreviation may be used provided:

(1) it is not identical with an abbreviation of weight or measure;

(2) it does not involve a drug with a generic name;

(3) there is no established abbreviation;

(4) it will not be confused with the symbol of an element or a group;

(5) the term is defined in a footnote, the text, or a glossary included at the end of the paper, according to the book or journal practice.

Abbreviations for specialized terms that appear frequently in a paper should generally be given in parentheses following first use of the full name (even if defined as under point 5 above). Thereafter the abbreviation may be used alone.

Symbols should be used in the text in such a way that their translation into words or phrases requires minimal effort on the part of the reader. Their meaning must always be unambiguous. Indiscriminate use of symbols may lead to cryptic writing, and authors should consider carefully the questions of style that arise from this practice.

Special attention must be given to the following recommendations on general principles concerning the use of symbols and abbreviations.

(1) A clear distinction is to be drawn between (a) symbols for physical quantities and (b) other symbols and abbreviations, including those denoting mathematical operations and constants, symbols for the chemical elements, and abbreviations for words and for the names of units.

Symbols for physical quantities normally consist of single letters of the Latin or the Greek alphabet with or without subscripts, superscripts, or other modifying signs. Where letters of the Latin alphabet (capitals or lower case) are used, they are to be printed in italic type. If a subscript is used, and the subscript itself represents a physical quantity, it will also be printed in italic type; otherwise the subscript will be in roman (upright) type.

C_g, C_p, typewritten as $\underline{C}_g$, $\underline{C}_p$

(g for gas phase, roman; p for pressure, a physical quantity, italic)

Boldface type will be used for vector quantities (*see also* p 33).

A, *a*, S, T, typewritten as $\underset{\sim}{\underline{A}}$, $\underset{\sim}{\underline{a}}$, $\underset{\sim}{\underline{S}}$, $\underset{\sim}{\underline{T}}$

Where letters of the Latin alphabet are used for other symbols and abbreviations as listed in (b), they will generally be printed in roman type.

(2) Chemical and mathematical copy should be precisely and carefully arranged. Haste and carelessness in the typing or drawing of symbols may lead to excessive cost and delay in later stages of publication through misinterpretation of the author's intent.

Letter symbols representing variables in mathematical expressions should be underlined for italics in the manuscript. This will avoid confusion with abbreviations or symbols for the chemical elements, which are to be set in roman type.

Symbols that may be difficult to interpret by editorial personnel or the printer are best explained in marginal pencil notes. Special attention should be given to Greek letters. Note that the capital Greek letters A, B, E, Z, H, I, K, M, N, O, P, T, and X are like certain English letters and may not be suitable as symbols. Greek letters that appear in a manuscript should not be underlined by the author.

Symbols for mathematical expressions are spaced just as the words that they represent would be spaced if written in ordinary language structure. Lack of spacing before and after symbols makes for delayed and confused reading just as would words without spacing. Exceptions are parentheses, brackets, braces, positive or negative quantities, and superscripts and subscripts. For example:

$a + b = c$ not $a+b=c$
$-x + y = z$ not $-x+y=z$
$e^{-(k+1)(x-t)}$ not $e^{-(k + 1)(x - t)}$

(3) Where it is necessary to select from alternative symbols for a quantity, or to adopt symbols for quantities for which there are no widely accepted specific symbols, consideration should be given to current practice by authorities in the field and to the desirability of adopting a single set of self-consistent symbols. The author must then define clearly in the paper all terms and units. The selected symbols should permit modification in accordance with a uniform scheme for the representation of any important series of corresponding derived quantities. They should also be symbols that are available in most composition systems. (If a paper will be replete with difficult notation, the author should, before devising his notation, consult the Editorial Department concerning the feasibility of setting complex expressions and the availability of special characters.)

(4) The same abbreviation or symbol is applicable to either the singular or the plural form of the word.

(5) *Most abbreviations are used without periods.* Periods should always be omitted after symbols representing the names of units and physical quantities except where this cannot be done without causing ambiguity. However, it is customary to use a period after initials in the name of a person, after abbreviations of Latin expressions (i.e., etc., cf.), and when the abbreviation formed is itself a word (atomic, at; therefore, at. is used).

(6) Symbols and abbreviations denoting mathematical operations and constants should follow the standard practice of mathematicians.

(7) There are no rigid rules for the use of modifying signs such as subscripts, superscripts, and brackets, but a satisfactory notation should:
   (a) be unambiguous;
   (b) be systematic, simple, and easy to remember;
   (c) not use more letters and characters than necessary.

For example, where a subscript has to be added to a symbol that already carries a subscript, the two subscripts should be separated by a comma.

i.e., $a_{Na,R}$

In thermochemical work, an equation such as

$$Ag(s) + H^+(aq) + Cl^-(aq) = AgCl(s) + \tfrac{1}{2}H_2(g)$$

is preferable with full-size letters and parentheses. The form

$$Ag_{(s)} + H^+_{(aq)} + Cl^-_{(aq)} = AgCl_{(s)} + \tfrac{1}{2}H_{2(g)}$$

involves more effort and lends little to interpretation. Ease of composition, space requirements, and hyphenation difficulties should be factors in choosing superscripts and subscripts (composition rules forbid hyphenation in superscripts and subscripts; however, when the superscripts or subscripts are lengthy, forced line breaks to prevent this hyphenation will interfere with good word spacing).

Typing superscripts and subscripts requires special attention: superscripts directly over subscripts should be avoided. Consistent and meaningful sequence of subscripts and superscripts when both occur in the same expression should be observed.

(8) Brackets, including parentheses ( ), braces { }, and square brackets [ ], should not be used around the symbol for a quantity to make it represent any other quantity unless such use is consistently adopted for an entire class of quantities, as.in crystallography. Square brackets, [ ], enclosing a formula of a chemical species are used to indicate its concentration. Square brackets are also used to denote coordination entities.

In crystallography it is recommended that: Miller indices be enclosed in parentheses, ( ); Laue indices be unenclosed; indices of a form be enclosed in braces, { }; indices of a zone axis or line be enclosed in square brackets, [ ]. A symbol such as 123 or hkl is understood to be a reflection; (123) or (hkl) a plane or set of planes, [123] or $[uvw]$ a direction, $\{hkl\}$ a form, and $\langle uvw \rangle$ all crystallographically equivalent directions of the type $[uvw]$.

Specific Usages

International communication in science continues to grow in importance. The International Union of Pure and Applied Chemistry (IUPAC) and the International Union of Biochemistry (IUB) are concerned with academic and industrial aspects of chemistry for which international agreement and uniform practice are desirable. Examples are nomenclature, atomic weights, symbols and terminology, physico-chemical constants, and methods of analysis and assay. IUPAC and IUB, through their Divisions, Sections, and Commissions, serve as international forums where the views of outstanding specialists in many fields of chemical interest are presented, discussed, and, after approval, published. The American Chemical Society through its Committee on Nomenclature also contributes to the IUPAC and IUB work.

The preferred usages for symbols and abbreviations for the Society's books and journals are presented on the following pages. These examples are based on IUPAC and IUB recommendations.

SYMBOLS FOR PHYSICAL AND CHEMICAL QUANTITIES

A physical quantity is the product of a numerical value (a pure number) and a unit. Symbols for physical quantities should be single letters of the Latin or Greek alphabets; if Latin, the letter should be printed in italic type; therefore, it should be underlined on the manuscript. Occasionally two-letter symbols are used (e.g., in transport numbers). When such symbols appear as factors in a product, they should be enclosed in parentheses or separated from other factors by a space or a mathematical sign.

Subscripts or superscripts that are themselves symbols for physical quantities should be italicized; all others should be in roman type.

C_p, typewritten as $\underline{C}_p$, for heat capacity at constant pressure
C_B, typewritten as $\underline{C}_B$, for heat capacity of substance B.

The symbols for vector quantities should be printed in boldface italic type, e.g., A, a, typewritten and marked $\underline{A}$, $\underline{a}$, and tensors of the second rank should be printed in boldface roman type, e.g., S, T, typewritten as $\underset{\sim}{S}$, $\underset{\sim}{T}$.

When a chemical quantity is used in an equation, it is indicated by a single letter of the Latin alphabet, in italic type, or by placing the symbol of the substance in brackets or parentheses.

A list of commonly used symbols is given in Appendix B.

SYMBOLS OF CHEMICAL ELEMENTS, NUCLIDES, PARTICLES, AND SYSTEMS

Symbols for chemical elements should be written in roman type. The symbol is not followed by a period.

Ca, C, H, He

In accordance with IUPAC recommendation, a nuclide (species of atoms, each of which has identical atomic (proton) and mass (nucleon) number) may be specified by attaching numbers: mass number, left superscript position; atomic number, left subscript; number of atoms per molecule, right subscript; ionic charge, state of excitation, or oxidation number, right superscript. The atomic number is omitted in most cases. (In American Chemical Society publications the number of atoms and the ionic charge designations are staggered.)

$$_{16}^{32}\text{S}\,_2^{2+}$$

mass number ^{12}C, $^{35}\text{Cl}^-$

atomic number: $_6\text{C}$

ionic charge: Na^+, NO_3^-, Ca^{2+}, PO_4^{3-}, $^7\text{Li}^-$
(ionic charge should be indicated by a superscript plus or minus sign following the symbol of the ion; for multiple charges an Arabic superscript numeral should precede the plus or minus sign)

excited electronic state: He^*, NO^*

oxidation number: $\text{Pb}^{\text{II}}_2\text{Pb}^{\text{IV}}\text{O}_4$, $(\text{NH}_3)_2\text{Pt}^{\text{II}}$

The oxidation number of an element may also be indicated by a Roman numeral on the line and in parentheses. In formulas, the oxidation number should be superscript, without parentheses, as shown above.

cobalt(III) or Co(III); ferrate(−II)

In the formula of a free radical, the unshared electron may be indicated by a point in the middle position.

$\text{H}_3\text{C}\cdot$, $\text{C}_6\text{H}_5\cdot$, $\text{HO}\cdot$

A centered period (center dot) is also used when chemical formulas of addition compounds are given.

$\text{Na}_2\text{SO}_4\cdot10\text{H}_2\text{O}$, $\text{BH}_3\cdot\text{NH}_3$

Cation radicals and anion radicals should be indicated by the symbol, formula, or structure with the appropriate plus or minus followed by a center dot.

$\text{R}^+\cdot$, $\text{R}^{2+}\cdot$, $\text{R}^-\cdot$, $\text{R}^{2-}\cdot$

Bonds, single or multiple, should not be indicated by dots.
The mass number of an isotope should be used as a superior prefix (left superscript) only to an atomic symbol, not to an abbreviation.

[^{32}P]CMP, not CM^{32}P (P in CMP represents phosphate)
^{32}PO$_4{}^{3-}$
[2-^{14}C]leucine
(^{15}N)ammonia (isotopic substitution)
[^{15}N]alanine (isotopic labeling)

Symbols for particles and quanta are:

neutron	n	pion	π
proton	p	muon	μ
deuteron	d	electron	e
triton	t	neutrino	ν
helion	h	photon	γ
particle	x		

Electric charges are indicated by the appropriate superscript ($+$, $-$, 0; e.g., n^0, e$^+$, e$^-$). If the symbols p and e are used without indication of charge, they refer to positive proton and negative electron, respectively.

The meaning of abbreviated notations for nuclear reactions should be the following:

$$\text{initial nuclide} \begin{pmatrix} \text{incoming} & \text{outgoing} \\ \text{particle(s),} & \text{particle(s)} \\ \text{or quanta,} & \text{or quanta} \end{pmatrix} \text{final nuclide}$$

Examples:

$$^{14}\text{N}(\alpha,\text{p})^{17}\text{O} \qquad\qquad ^{59}\text{Co}(\text{n},\gamma)^{60}\text{Co}$$
$$^{23}\text{Na}(\gamma,3\text{n})^{20}\text{Na} \qquad\qquad ^{31}\text{P}(\gamma,\text{pn})^{29}\text{Si}$$

The quantum state of a system should be printed in roman type, capital letters; for a single particle, use lower case roman type

$L, l =$ 0: S,s
          1: P,p
          2: D,d
          3: F,f
          4: G,g
         11: O,o

A right subscript indicates the total angular momentum quantum number J or j. A left superscript indicates the spin multiplicity $2S + 1$.

^{2}P$_{3/2}$ (state)
p$_{3/2}$ (electron)

Atomic electron configurations are indicated by $(nl)^k(n'l')^{k'}$. For specific configurations, the appropriate substitutions are made:

$(1s)^2(2s)^2(2p)^3(3s)^1$

SYMBOLS AND ABBREVIATIONS FOR
CHEMICAL AND BIOCHEMICAL COMPOUNDS

The limited use of abbreviations and symbols of specified meaning for the names of chemical substances is accepted, especially in instances that would otherwise require the repeated use of unwieldy terms. However, clarity and unambiguity are more important than brevity. In titles, abbreviations should be avoided. In abstracts, they should be kept to a minimum, and only standard abbreviations (*see below*) may be used without definition.

Compounds listed and described in a paper should be numbered by boldface Arabic numerals. When referring to numbered compounds, parentheses are used when the compound number is not really necessary but simply aids in identification; parentheses are not used where the number is essential.

Four grams of 11β-hydroxyprogesterone (**4**) was dissolved . . .

Compound **2** was treated with . . .

The oxidation product contained a keto alcohol, **3**, that . . .

(There is often a disparity between numbering of compounds in a primary journal and numbering of the same compounds in an abstract published by a secondary service. In some primary journal articles it is not unusual to have several tens or hundreds of compounds; only a few of these would be mentioned in an abstract. In the abstract appearing in *Chemical Abstracts,* compounds would be numbered in sequence and with Roman numerals starting with I; the numbers would not correlate with similar numbers in the journal, only with the structures or compound designations given in the abstract.)

Nonstandard (*standard* means established by official recommendations) abbreviations and symbols should not conflict with standard forms or with the general principles proposed in nomenclature rules. Nonstandard abbreviations should *always* be defined in each paper.

As many of the recommendations for abbreviations presented in the nomenclature reports covering the various areas of chemistry should be followed as is possible in the light of individual circumstances (*see* Chemical Nomenclature). A few of these recommendations have been selected and are presented in the following list.

(1) The prefixes cis, trans, sym, asym should be connected with the chemical formula by a hyphen, and they should be italicized.

cis-[PtCl$_2$(NH$_3$)$_2$]

(2) The stoichiometric proportions may be denoted by prefixes, such as mono, di, tri, bis, tris, preceding without hyphen the names of the elements or groups to which they refer. These prefixes are not italicized.

N$_2$S$_5$, dinitrogen pentasulfide
[Co(H$_2$NCH$_2$CH$_2$NH$_2$)$_3$]Cl$_3$, tris(ethylenediamine)cobalt(III)
   chloride

(3) The proportions of the constituents in a formula also may be indicated indirectly by Stock's system, that is, by Roman numerals representing the oxidation state of the element, placed in parentheses immediately following the name. For zero, the Arabic 0 should be used. When used in conjunction with symbols, the Roman number may be placed above and to the right. When a combination of symbols is used, the numeral should be expressed as a superscript without parentheses. The Stock notation can be applied to both cations and anions.

FeCl$_2$, iron(II) chloride
MnO$_2$, manganese(IV) oxide
K$_4$[Ni(CN)$_4$], potassium tetracyanonickelate(0)
[Cr(H$_2$O)$_6$](ClO$_4$)$_3$, hexaaquachromium(III) perchlorate
(NH$_3$)$_2$Pt^{II}, diammineplatinum(II)

(4) In di- and polynuclear compounds, a bridging group should be indicated by adding the Greek letter μ immediately before its name and separating the unit from the rest of the complex by a hyphen. Two or more bridging groups of the same kind are indicated by di-μ-, etc. A subscript is used to designate multiplicity when a bridging group is linked to more than two nuclear centers.

Be$_4$O(CH$_3$COO)$_6$, μ_4-oxo-hexa-μ-acetato-tetraberyllium

(5) For chemical purposes, polymorphs should be indicated by adding the crystal system after the name or formula.

ZnS(cub) = zinc blende or sphalerite
ZnS(hex) = wurtzite

(6) In general, configurational relationships should be denoted by capital italic Roman letter prefixes R and S. The RS system is based on the actual three-dimensional formula of the compound to be named.

In carbohydrate and amino acid nomenclature, configurational relationships are usually denoted by the small capital Roman letter prefixes D and L.

The optical rotational sign under specified conditions is indicated by (+) or (−). Racemic modifications may be indicated by the prefixes DL, *dl,* or (±). Where applicable, the prefix *meso-* is used.

D-glucose or D(+)-glucose

(7) Certain specialized symbols and abbreviations are permitted without definition in several journals. Specific recommendations for specialized nomenclature may be found in the instructions to authors published in each journal.

Special symbols, although they may be fairly common, should be defined in any paper if it is thought that readers might be unfamiliar with them.

ABBREVIATIONS FOR WORDS OTHER THAN NAMES OF UNITS

Abbreviations and Symbols Permitted without Identification

(1) Symbols for amino acids (these symbols should not be used for a single amino acid residue except in the restricted sense of sequence identification, e.g., Glu-248. They should be used only in sequences or in formulating derivatives.)

(2) Symbols for chemical elements (*see* Appendix B)

(3) Symbols for groups or radicals

Ac	acetyl
Bu (*n*-Bu, *sec*-Bu, *i*-Bu, *t*-Bu)	butyl (*n*-butyl, *sec*-butyl, isobutyl, *tert*-butyl)
Bz	benzoyl
Et	ethyl
Me	methyl
Ph	phenyl
Pr (*i*-Pr, c-Pr)	propyl (isopropyl, cyclopropyl)

(4) abbreviations for the following terms

atomic weight	at. wt
boiling point	bp
chemically pure	CP
circa (about)	ca.
confer (compare)	cf.

edited, edition	ed.
Editor	Ed.
equivalent weight	equiv wt
et alii (and others)	et al.
et cetera	etc.
exempli gratia (for example)	e.g.
freezing point	fp
ibidem (in the same place)	ibid.
id est (that is)	i.e.
infrared	IR
melting point	mp
mixture melting point	mmp
moles per liter (concentration)	M
molecular weight (relative molecular mass)	M_r
mole percent	mol %
nuclear magnetic resonance	NMR
percent	%
reference(s)	ref
specific heat	sp ht
specific volume	sp vol
ultraviolet	UV
United States Pharmacopeia	USP
versus	vs.
volume	vol
volume per volume	v/v
weight	wt
weight per weight	w/w

Abbreviations and Symbols for Which Definition May Be Necessary

This list is not meant to be exhaustive, merely representative; thus AMP appears, but not ADP and ATP or abbreviations for the other nucleotides. AES is given; AFS (atomic fluorescence spectroscopy) is formed in the same way and subject to the same restrictions and recommendations. ENDOR is defined; INDOR is formed and defined similarly.

Abbreviations and symbols of the forms below may be commonplace in certain fields. Individual books and journals, in their instructions to authors, may list specific abbreviations that are acceptable without definition.

Acronyms that are listed in the "Chemical Abstracts Service Index Guide" (see Bibliography) may be used with proper definition.

AAS   atomic absorption spectroscopy
ACTH   adrenocorticotropin

AES	atomic emission spectroscopy
af	audio frequency
AMP	adenosine 5'-phosphate (M, monophosphate)
AO	atomic orbital
ATR	attenuated total reflection
BOD	biological oxygen demand
bpy	2,2'-bipyridine(-dyl)
cAMP	adenosine 3',5'-cyclic monophosphate
Cbz	carbobenzyloxy; benzyloxycarbonyl
CD	circular dichroism
CE	Cotton effect
CI	chemical ionization
	configuration interaction
CIDEP	chemically induced dynamic electron polarization
cmc	critical micelle concentration
CNDO	complete neglect of differential overlap
Cp	cyclopentadienyl
CPE	controlled potential electrolysis
CPL	circular polarization of luminescence
cRNA	complementary ribonucleic acid
CRT	cathode ray tube
CRU	constitutional repeating unit
CT	charge transfer
CW	continuous wave
Dabco	1,4-diazabicyclo[2.2.2]octane
dAMP	2'-deoxyadenosine 5'-phosphate
dc	direct current
DSC	differential scanning calorimetry
DTA	differential thermal analysis
EFG	electric field gradient
EI	electron impact
	electron ionization
EF_{50}	effective dose—fifty
emf	electromotive force
EM	electron microscopy
ENDOR	electron (external) nuclear double resonance
EPR	electron paramagnetic resonance
ESCA	electron spectroscopy for chemical analysis
ESR	electron spin resonance
eu	entropy unit
FAD	flavin adenine dinucleotide
FAFS	flame atomic fluorescence spectroscopy
FI	field ionization
FT	Fourier transform

fwhm	full width at half-maximum
GC	gas chromatography
GLC	gas–liquid chromatography
Hb	hemoglobin
HOMO	highest occupied molecular orbital
ICR	ion cyclotron resonance
IE	ionization energy
IF_{50}	infective dose—fifty
INO	iterative natural orbital
IP	ionization potential
LCAO	linear combination of atomic orbitals
LD_{50}	lethal dose—fifty
LFER	linear free-energy relationship
LIS	lanthanide-induced shift
LUMO	lowest unoccupied molecular orbital
MR	molecular refraction
MS	mass spectroscopy
NAD	nicotinamide adenine dinucleotide
NOCOR	neglect of core orbitals
NOE	nuclear Overhauser effect
NQR	nuclear quadrupole resonance
ORD	optical rotatory dispersion
POPOP	1,4-bis[2-(5-phenyloxazolyl)]benzene
py	pyridine
SAR	structure–activity relationship
SCE	saturated calomel electrode
SCF	self-consistent field
STO	Slater-type orbital
Tempo	2,2,6,6-tetramethyl-1-piperidinyloxy
TLC	thin-layer chromatography
VPC	vapor pressure chromatography
VSIP	valence state ionization potential
XRD	X-ray diffraction
zfsc	zero-field splitting constant

Abbreviations and Symbols for Limited Use, without Definition

Conservation and effective utilization of space are particularly essential in preparing schemes, charts, equations, formulas, tables, figures. The following abbreviations (in addition to all symbols and abbreviations whose use is not restricted or proscribed) are recommended for this purpose, but their use in the text should be avoided. In addition, abbreviations appearing in the first issue of each volume of *Chemical Abstracts* are recommended (*see Chem. Abstr.* **1978,** *88*(1), xvii). (*CA* uses periods for abbreviations other than those of units; primary journals and books use abbreviations without periods.)

abs	absolute
anhyd	anhydrous
aq	aqueous
av	average
biol	biological(ly)
calcd	calculated
coeff	coefficient
compd	compound
concd	concentrated
concn	concentration
const	constant
cor	corrected
crit	critical
cryst	crystalline
decomp	decompose
diam	diameter
dil	dilute
distd	distilled
expt(l)	experiment(al)
(g), as in $H_2O(g)$	gas
insol	insoluble
(l), as in $H_2O(l)$	liquid
max	maximum
min	minimum
obsd	observed
ppt	precipitate
prepn	preparation
recryst	recrystallized
(s), as in $AgCl(s)$	solid
sol	soluble
soln	solution
std	standard
sym	symmetrical
temp, t (Celsius), T (kelvin)	temperature

Abbreviations Proscribed or Not Recommended

The chemical literature is replete with abbreviations. Too often, one abbreviation has multiple meanings (e.g., PMR: proton magnetic resonance, phosphorus magnetic resonance, paramagnetic resonance;

DMR, D for dynamic or ^{2}H). In addition, new abbreviations are coined and old abbreviations are retained despite recommendations for standard forms. Also some abbreviations potentially lend themselves to grammatical errors and redundancies (the ESCA spectra: electron spectroscopy for chemical analysis spectra; this is a common duplication of words). For these reasons, the following abbreviations should not be used for the definitions listed:

CMR	^{13}C magnetic resonance (use ^{13}C NMR)
DMR	^{2}H magnetic resonance (use ^{2}H NMR)
DMSO	dimethyl sulfoxide (use Me$_2$SO)
FIR (or fir)	far-infrared (use far-IR)
FTS	Fourier transform spectroscopy (use FT spectroscopy)
MIR (or mir)	mid-infrared (use mid-IR)
NIR (or nir)	near-infrared (use near-IR)
PMR	proton or phosphorus magnetic resonance (use ^{1}H or ^{31}P NMR)
TMS	tetramethylsilane (use Me$_4$Si) trimethylsilyl (use Me$_3$Si)
VUV (or vuv)	vacuum ultraviolet (use vacuum-UV)

SYSTEMS OF UNITS

Before the 1960s, four systems of units were commonly used in the scientific literature: the English System (centuries old, using yard and pound), the Metric System (dating from the 18th century, with meter and kilogram as standard units), the CGS System (based on the metric, with the centimeter, gram, and second being base units), and the MKSA or Giorgi System (meter, kilogram, second, and ampere are base units).

The International System of Units (SI, Système International) is the most recent effort to develop a coherent system of units. It is "coherent" because all units within the framework are derived from a restricted set of independently defined base units by simple multiplication or division. It is coherent also in the sense that it has been adopted as a universal system to facilitate communication of numerical data and to restrict proliferation of systems.

SI is an extension and simplification of the metric system. Its principal features were adopted in 1954 by the 10th General Conference on Weights and Measures (GCWM); its full title, International System of Units, was given in 1960 by the 11th GCWM. Increased precision of measurement and sophistication of equipment have caused and will continue to cause modifications (further improvements were made in 1964, 1968, 1971, and 1975).

SI is constructed from seven base units for independent quantities plus two supplementary units for plane and solid angle: meter, kilogram, second, ampere, kelvin, mole, candela, radian, and steradian. Most physicochemical measurements can be expressed in terms of these units.

Papers submitted to journals of the American Chemical Society should use SI. A discussion of SI and tables of units are given in Appendix A; alphabetical lists of SI units and accompanying prefixes are given in Tables I–III. However, certain units not part of SI are so widely used that it is impractical to abandon them (for example, liter, minute, hour) or so well established that the International Committee for Weights and Measures has authorized, for a limited time, their continued use (e.g., curie, roentgen, ångström; see Appendix A). These exceptions are permitted in ACS books and journals. In addition, quantities that are expressed in terms of the fundamental constants of

Table I: SI Units[a]

unit	symbol	physical quantity
ampere	A	electric current
becquerel	Bq	activity (of radionuclide)
candela	cd	luminous intensity
coulomb	C	quantity of electricity, electric charge
farad	F	capacitance
gray	Gy	absorbed dose
henry	H	inductance
hertz	Hz	frequency
joule	J	energy, work, quantity of heat
kelvin	K	thermodynamic temperature
kilogram	kg	mass
lumen	lm	luminous flux
lux	lx	illuminance
meter	m	length
mole	mol	amount of substance
newton	N	force
ohm	Ω	electric resistance
pascal	Pa	pressure, stress
radian	rad	plane angle
second	s	time
siemens	S	conductance
steradian	sr	solid angle
tesla	T	magnetic flux density
volt	V	electric potential, potential difference, electromotive force
watt	W	power, radiant flux
weber	Wb	magnetic flux

[a] Expressions of SI derived units in terms of base units are given in Appendix A. SI base units are italicized, and SI supplementary units are boldfaced.

Table II: Examples of SI Derived Units Expressed in Terms of Base Units or by Special Names

acceleration	meter per second squared	m/s^2
area	square meter	m^2
concentration (of amount of substance)	mole per cubic meter	mol/m^3 [a]
current density	ampere per square meter	A/m^2
density, mass density	kilogram per cubic meter	kg/m^3
dynamic viscosity	pascal second	$Pa \cdot s$
electric charge density	coulomb per cubic meter	C/m^3
electric field strength	volt per meter	V/m
electric flux density	coulomb per square meter	C/m^2
energy density	joule per cubic meter	J/m^3
heat capacity, entropy	joule per kelvin	J/K
heat flux density, irradiance	watt per square meter	W/m^2
luminance	candela per square meter	cd/m^2
magnetic field strength	ampere per meter	A/m
molar energy	joule per mole	J/mol
molar entropy, molar heat capacity	joule per mole kelvin	$J/(mol \cdot K)$
moment of force	newton meter	$N \cdot m$
permeability	henry per meter	H/m
permittivity	farad per meter	F/m
specific energy	joule per kilogram	J/kg
specific heat capacity, specific entropy	joule per kilogram kelvin	$J/(kg \cdot K)$
specific volume	cubic meter per kilogram	m^3/kg
speed, velocity	meter per second	m/s
surface tension	newton per meter	N/m
thermal conductivity	watt per meter kelvin	$W/(m \cdot K)$
volume	cubic meter	m^3 [a]
wavenumber	one per meter	m^{-1}

[a] Liter (L) is a special name for cubic decimeter. When concentration is expressed as moles per cubic decimeter, the symbol M for the term molar concentration may be used.

Table III: Multiplicative Prefixes[a]

factor	prefix	symbol	factor	prefix	symbol
10^{-18}	atto	a	10^1	deka	da
10^{-15}	femto	f	10^2	hecto	h
10^{-12}	pico	p	10^3	kilo	k
10^{-9}	nano	n	10^6	mega	M
10^{-6}	micro	μ	10^9	giga	G
10^{-3}	milli	m	10^{12}	tera	T
10^{-2}	centi	c	10^{15}	peta	P
10^{-1}	deci	d	10^{18}	exa	E

[a] Any of these prefixes may be combined with any of the symbols permitted within SI. Thus, kPa and GPa will both be common combinations in measurements of pressure and stress, as will mL and cm for measurements of volume and length. As a general rule, however, the prefix chosen should be 10 raised to that multiple of 3 that will bring the numerical value of the quantity to a positive value less than 1000.

nature (units such as elementary charge, proton mass, Bohr magneton, speed of light, Planck constant) are acceptable providing the author clearly states which natural units are being used; broad terms such as "atomic units" should be avoided.

Guides on Use of SI

(1) Capitalization. When written in full, the names of all units start with a lower case letter. When symbols are used, the symbol can be either lower case or capital or a combination of the two. In no case should the symbol be altered (changing a capital to a lower case letter can make it a different symbol—s, S, for example, second and siemens—or introduce a large error into data in the case of multiplicative prefixes—m, M, for example, milli and mega).

(2) Plurals. When written in full, the names of units are made plural when appropriate (fractions less than one are always singular). Symbols are the same whether singular or plural.

(3) Periods. Symbols should not have periods.

(4) Numbers. Numbers containing more than four digits preceding or following the decimal should be separated into groups of three, starting from the decimal point. (In tables, the column of data should dictate adherence to or deviation from this recommendation. With most numbers grouped, four-digit numbers should also be grouped; with most numbers solid, five- or six-digit numbers should not be grouped. *See* Numbers and Mathematical Expressions, (9), for an example. In equations, numbers should be written without spaces.)

(5) Spacing. Symbols should be spaced from the numbers to which they refer. Combinations of multiplicative prefixes and units should be written as one word or one symbol (kilojoule or kJ).

(6) Compound Units. Symbols for compound units should be written using a center dot for multiplication and a solidus or negative exponent for division (watt per meter kelvin, $W/(m \cdot K)$, $W \cdot (m \cdot K)^{-1}$, or $W \cdot m^{-1} \cdot K^{-1}$; consistency within the paper is necessary).

(7) Mixed Words and Symbols. Do not mix words and symbols (J per mole is prohibited; use J/mol, $J \, mol^{-1}$, $J \cdot mol^{-1}$, or joules per mole). When numbers are used, symbols should also be used (10 joules per mole is not permitted; the expression should read $10 \, J/mol$, $10 \, J \, mol^{-1}$, or $10 \, J \cdot mol^{-1}$; note that the center dot separates parts of a compound unit, but the exponent refers only to one unit; if the exponent is meant to refer to both, the expression would be $(J \cdot mol)^{-1}$ or $J^{-1} \cdot mol^{-1}$).

In some specialized fields (e.g., magnetism in material media), the appropriate quantities are still to be determined. Introducing conversion factors may be misleading, so flexibility is required. SI would be used whenever the appropriate guidelines are adopted. The American National Metric Council and the National Bureau of Standards publicize recommendations and offer advice on all aspects of conversion to SI.

Until the use of SI over other systems is dominant, exceptions will vary depending on the journal and will be discussed in the various instructions to authors.

Chemical Nomenclature

Good chemical nomenclature is essential for effective scientific communication. Authors should be aware that faulty or poor nomenclature seriously handicaps the communication of their achievements to the scientific community. In a field in which perhaps as many as five million chemical substances are known (over four million substances have been recorded in the Chemical Abstracts Service (CAS) Registry System since it began in 1965) and over 350 000 new substances are reported each year, the need is obvious for clear, unambiguous, and complete identification of each substance in the primary literature. Using ambiguous names or poorly defined nomenclature practices can result in the loss of the record of the actual compound: it may not be retrievable from the secondary literature. Trade names, acronyms, laboratory codes, and symbols should be avoided in titles. Acronyms and symbols, if used in the text, should be defined clearly and unambiguously (*see* Abbreviations, Symbols, and Units).

The Chemical Abstracts Service must use a single, unique index name for each substance. This is required in its highly organized indexes, that collect in one location substances of similar molecular composition. However, authors of articles in the primary literature do not face this rigorous restriction. CAS index names may not be the best descriptors for the substances of interest in a particular study. Nevertheless, a substance name used in a primary paper should (a) describe the chemical structure unambiguously or (b) be widely recognized in scientific fields. It should ideally conform to the rules established by the appropriate international organization, the recommendations made by the American Chemical Society Committee on Nomenclature, and/or the nomenclature recommendations and practices of the Chemical Abstracts Service.

Chemical names for drugs should be used. In cases where the terminology is unwieldy, generic names, if available, may be used throughout the manuscript after the first mention and identification. Formally adopted generic names are listed in United States Adopted Names (USAN). Trade names and laboratory codes should not be used except as additional information. (Trade names, when used, are spelled with an initial capital and subsequent lower case letters. The symbol ® is not used with trademarks.) Authors should avoid assuming that any given name is widely known and should not rely on references to previously published articles for identification. Descriptions of stereochemistry, location of labeled atoms, and similar information should be exact and clearly understandable. Systems of nomenclature should not be mixed. (For example, the series of alcohols methyl, ethyl, propyl, isopropyl, n-butyl, sec-butyl, isobutyl, tert-butyl should not be mixed with the entries from the comparable series methanol, ethanol, 1- and 2-propanol, 1-butanol, 2-butanol, 2-methyl-1-propanol (not isobutanol), 2-methyl-2-propanol (never tert-butanol). The first set follows radicofunctional terminology; the second, substitutive nomenclature.)

Chemical nomenclature has a long history of development beginning formally with the Geneva Conference of 1892. As the sophistication of scientific techniques increased, as new types and classes of compounds were discovered, and as scientists became interested in discussing theoretical substances, the need for refining and extending chemical nomenclature rules became more and more acute.

The American Chemical Society, through its Committee on Nomenclature, cooperates with national and international organizations active in chemical and related fields. These associations include the several Nomenclature Commissions of the International Union of Pure and Applied Chemistry (IUPAC), the IUPAC–IUB Commission on Biochemical Nomenclature, and various committees of the divisions of the American Chemical Society. An annotated bibliography of chemical nomenclature publications of these organizations and other interested individuals and groups is included in the Chemical Abstracts Service "Index Guide" for Volume 88 (1978), §§295–306. These instructions also outline the procedures by which CAS derives its unique index names for a variety of classes of substances. Extremely valuable additional references are the publications of the International Union of Pure and Applied Chemistry—"Nomenclature of Inorganic Chemistry, 1970"; Butterworths: London, 1971; "Nomenclature of Organic Chemistry, Sections A, B & C"; Butterworths: London, 1971; "Section D" (Organic Compounds Containing Elements Which are not exclusively Carbon, Hydrogen, Oxygen, Nitrogen, Halogen, Sulfur, Selenium and Tellurium), 1973; "Section E" (Stereochemistry), 1968; "Section F" (Natural Products and Related Compounds), 1976—as well as "Nomenclature of Organic Compounds: Principles and Practice"; Adv. Chem. Ser. 1974, No. 126.

Authors may obtain assistance with their nomenclature problems by contacting: The Director of Nomenclature, Chemical Abstracts Service, P.O. Box 3012, Columbus, OH 43210.

Preparation and Presentation of Special Sections

EXPERIMENTAL DETAILS

Clarity and brevity are extremely important. The publication's preferences concerning abbreviations, symbols, punctuation, and spacing should be closely followed.

Materials and equipment should be described in sufficient detail to enable others to repeat the experiment. Novel experimental procedures should be thoroughly discussed, but published procedures should be referred to only by literature citation. Modifications to established procedures, when pertinent, should be included. General reaction conditions should be given only once. If a table or a figure caption is the most appropriate location, avoid duplication elsewhere. Instruments used as well as standard techniques and procedures applicable throughout the work should appear in a paragraph at the beginning of the section. When computer programs are used, give a reference to the source of the program.

Before selecting a notation, consider whether the notation can be followed by the printer. A good rule of thumb is: if the material cannot be typed, the symbol(s) may not be available in the composition process. If this may be the case, consult with the Books or the Editorial Department on the availability of various characters and the feasibility of using various accents. Notations requiring hand operations will not be permitted in journals; foresight could eliminate the need for extensive revision.

The title of an experiment (normally given as a paragraph-indented side head, printed in boldface or italic type), when applicable, should include the chemical name and compound number of the product prepared; subsequently this compound should be identified by number. Symbols or chemical formulas for simple chemicals are encouraged. Symbols should be used exclusively for peptides containing more than three amino acid residues and for nucleosides and nucleotides containing multiple purine and pyrimidine bases. (Arginylphenylalanine is sufficiently difficult to read; anything longer, such as arginylvalyl-phenylalanine, hinders comprehension. In the protein field, use of symbols facilitates understanding; note the clarity of the form Arg-Val-Phe. Again, symbols increase comprehension and avoid cumbersome construction in nucleic acid work. Consider pA-C-U-dT-dG vs. phosphoadenylyl(3′–5′)cytidylyl(3′–5′)uridylyl(3′–5′)thymidylyl(3′–5′)deoxyguanosine 5′-phosphate.) As long as the symbols chosen convey meaning to those moderately familiar with the field and the meaning of the symbols is suitably referenced for those less familiar, they are valuable tools in effective communication.

Hazardous operations or use of toxic compounds demands special attention (in the form of **Caution:** followed by the reason).

The guidelines below should be followed in preparing experimental sections of papers.

(1) Data characterizing compounds should, in general, be presented as shown in the following example:

"The ethereal extract was dried ($MgSO_4$), concentrated, and distilled, giving 10.23 g (65%) of the acetoxy ketone **12:** bp 82–83 °C (0.4 kPa[1]); n^{25}_D 1.4266 [lit.[6] bp 80–82 °C (0.5 kPa), n^{25}_D 1.4261]; d^{25}_4 0.823; $[\alpha]^{25}_D$ +10.0° (c 6, CH_3OH); UV max (95% C_2H_5OH) 275 mm (ϵ 21.3), 246 (11 720), 220 (5150); IR (CCl_4) 1725 and 1740 (ester C=O), 1724 (acetyl C=O) cm^{-1}; NMR (CCl_4) δ 45.1 (d, 1, $J_{5,6}$ = 8.5 Hz), 3.98 (t, 2, J = 6 Hz, CH_2OAc), 3.5–3.85 (m, 3, C_4 H and C_5 H), 3.46 (br s, 1, C_3 H), 2.43 (t, 3, J = 6 Hz, CH_2CO), 2.07 (s, 3), 1.97 (s, 3), and 1.6 (m, 4); mass spectrum, m/z (rel intensity) 158 (5), 115 (6), 100 (50), 99 (11), 98 (100), 85 (10)."

Note in this example the use or nonuse of the equal sign (ϵ 21.3; J = 6 Hz). In general, equal signs are used with calculated values (pK = 2.2) but not with values obtained by reading an instrument (pH 3.2). However, the equal sign is necessary for any expression in which it (=) is the verb. Note also the avoidance of structural formulas (acetyl); only linear formulas or fragments are permitted. If it is necessary to convey structural information, the structure should be set off and labeled (A, B, or i, ii, etc.), and the label should be used in the text. Stereochemical information can be given by the appropriate descriptors ((Z)-HC=CH, e.g.).

In NMR descriptions, s = singlet, d = doublet, t = triplet, m = multiplet, br = broad.

(2) Combustion analyses. Authors should consult the instructions to authors of a journal for requirements regarding combustion analyses and format for reporting these data. For those journals whose instructions do not discuss the subject, the following form should be used:

Anal. Calcd for $C_{10}H_{15}NO_7$: C, 45.98; H, 5.79; N, 5.36. Found: C, 46.02; H, 5.86; N, 5.35.

Amino acid analyses (ratios) should be indicated as: $His_{0.9}$-$Glu_{1.1}Val_{1.1}Leu_{1.9}$.

(3) Spectra. Ultraviolet, infrared, magnetic resonance, or mass spectra will be reproduced in journals only if they are essential to establish a conclusion or permit detailed interpretation. (Books routinely reproduce spectra.) Otherwise, spectral data should be presented in

---

[1] 1 mmHg = 0.1333 kPa; 1 atm = 101.325 kPa.

numerical form in the experimental part, or in exceptional cases in tables or miniprint form, or as supplementary material for inclusion in the microform editions of the journal. For those papers dealing primarily with interpretation of spectra and those in which bond shape or fine structure illustrations are necessary, the appropriate figures will be published. Routine spectral data should be summarized as illustrated above (1).

The same requirements apply to gas chromatographic data.

In preparing copy for reproduction of spectra, the general rules for illustrations apply. When spectra are to be presented in the same form as actually recorded, photographic reproductions of experimental spectra or accurate tracings are preferable. Photocopies of spectra are seldom of adequate quality for use by the printer. Only the pertinent part of a spectrum should be shown. The scale on the abscissa (and ordinate if pertinent) should be shown and should be consistent with units used in the paper. If structural formulas are included on spectra, drawing and lettering must be carefully done. In bar graphs of mass spectra, m/z values of principal peaks should be lettered in on the graph; white space in such graphs can be advantageously used to denote fragmentation patterns. Experimental conditions may be specified in figure legends or in the text as appropriate (not both).

For a group of similar compounds with insignificant differences in their spectra, presentation of one spectrum is sufficient.

(4) Some types of data can be presented in the running text much more concisely than in tabular form. For instance, values of vapor pressure as a function of temperature can be given as a series of T (K), P (kPa) values as in the example:

"Values of the vapor pressure of the compound, measured over a range of temperature, are [given as T (K), P (kPa)]: 175.5, 0.0133; 189.7, 0.0798; 209.8, 0.319; 228.1, 1.33; 250.4, 5.32; 273.3, 21.92; and 299.3, 50.86."

(5) Reports of crystal structure analyses in conjunction with chemical studies are encouraged. These reports should conform to recommendations of the Commission on Crystallographic Data of the International Union of Crystallography [*Acta Crystallogr.* **1967,** *22,* 445; *see also Acta Crystallogr. Sect. A* **1973,** *29,* Part 1, 1, for specific details on size and arrangement of material and a checklist of important information]. In particular, a tabulation of F_o and F_c should be appended. The results and analysis should include: (1) unit cell parameters and standard errors; (2) the formula, formula weight, and number of formula units in the unit cell; (3) measured and calculated densities; (4) space group; (5) wavelength used, number of reflections observed, and (for diffractometer data) number of unobservedly weak reflections; (6) method of collection of intensity data and methods of structure solution and re-

finement (references may suffice); (7) final R value; (8) statement on the presence or absence of significant features on a final difference Fourier map; (9) *noteworthy* bond lengths and angles and/or a "three-dimensional" representation showing the salient structural features; (10) tables (with standard deviations) of (a) final atomic positional parameters, (b) atomic thermal parameters, (c) bond distances and angles.

The crystal structure factor tables will appear in the microfilm edition and on microfiche as supplementary material. For preparation instructions, *see* Microform Supplements.

If the data were collected with counter techniques, then, in addition to the recommendations of the Commission, a complete description of the type of instrument, type of scan, and method of handling background should be given.

Drawings of crystal or molecular structure should be made with the noncrystallographer in mind. Stereoscopic pairs of perspective drawings will be accepted (*see* Illustrations).

(6) Presentation of X-ray powder diffraction data for new material or materials previously uncharacterized by this technique is encouraged. Data from X-ray powder measurements should be accompanied by details of the experimental technique: the radiation, its wavelength, what filters or monochromators were used, camera diameter, the type of X-ray recording, and the technique for estimating intensities. Relevant information about the specimen used should be included. (Authors may wish to submit X-ray powder data to Mr. W. Frank McClune, Managing Editor, Powder Diffraction File, Joint Committee on Powder Diffraction Standards, 1601 Park Lane, Swarthmore, PA 19081. Standard forms for reporting the data are obtainable from Mr. McClune at the above address.)

(7) Computer programs should be given only in the detail necessary. If the program is an established procedure, a reference to its availability should suffice. If the algorithm is a modification of one in general use, a description of the modification should be deposited in an archival medium. One or more representative data sets or complete runs, so that complete details of the computations are available, should also be deposited. Sufficient information about programs and data should be provided so that others can repeat the calculations. The journals' supplementary material service (*see* Microform Supplements) is an appropriate medium for storing such details. In addition, the Quantum Chemistry Program Exchange (Indiana University, Bloomington, IN 47401) is concerned with disseminating computer software relating to chemistry. This Exchange has an archival aspect in that authors may deposit their programs, which then become available to the general public.

(8) In theoretical and computational papers, extensive tabulation of numerical results, such as electron populations, electron densities, magnitudes of atomic orbital coefficients, and detailed mathematical expositions, is often unnecessary. This material, if of sufficient interest, should be deposited as supplementary material (*see* Microform Supplements).

MICROFORM SUPPLEMENTS*

Manuscripts often contain extensive tables, graphs, spectra, mathematical derivations, computer algorithms, protein sequence analyses, multiple regression analyses, experimental material not central to, but bordering on, the central theme of the paper, expanded discussions of peripheral points, or other material which, though essential to the specialized reader, need not be elaborated in the paper itself. This material is made part of the permanent record by publication in the microfilm edition of the journal. In addition, the material is also provided on microfiche to subscribers of supplementary material (11 publications offer these subscriptions) or by special order, on microfiche and in photocopy, to any interested reader. The supplementary material is indexed by *Chemical Abstracts.*

Material submitted as supplementary material must be camera-ready copy. Economy of space should be the guiding principle. Single-spaced copy is therefore preferable. If the material is typewritten, a good ribbon and error-free copy are essential. If computer printouts are used, the printouts must be clear, with no broken letters, preferred character size 2.5 mm, optimum dimensions 22 × 28 cm. Detailed instructions for preparation of material to be microfilmed are outlined in Appendix F.

When tables are to appear as supplementary material, they should be grouped together to conserve space. When figures are submitted, they should be drafted on a small scale and mounted, in multiple, with accompanying captions on the same paper, 22 × 28 cm. India ink drawings are preferred, and matte prints should be used rather than glossies. (Because of the reproduction process involved, use of glossy prints may result in filmed material of nonuniform quality.)

Microform material should be submitted, in the appropriate number of copies and clearly labeled, with the original manuscript. After the paper is accepted, this material will be processed as is (unless the preparation requirements are not met), and proof will not be sent to authors.

* This section does not apply to publications of the Books Department.

Each paper containing microform material should have an explanatory paragraph at the end of the paper, giving a brief description of the nature and the amount of the material, as follows: "Supplementary Material Available: Spectra (^{1}H NMR) for compounds **3–10** (3 pages). Ordering information is given on any current masthead page." Any modification necessary will be introduced by the Editorial Department.

Authors who use other documentation services or depositories are encouraged to ask that this material, when relevant to the manuscript being considered for publication, be accepted as supplementary material. It will then become part of the permanent archives of the American Chemical Society by being included immediately following the article itself in the microfilm issue of the journal.

Inquiries concerning: the type of material suitable for archiving should be directed to the editor or managing editor of the journal involved; format and style, to the Editorial Department, Books and Journals Division; subscriptions to microfiche, to Microforms Program, Books and Journals Division; and individual orders for supplementary material, to Business Operations, Books and Journals Division.

MINIPRINT MATERIAL*

"Miniprint" is an effort to conserve journal space by special treatment of material that is of marginal interest to many readers, but of sufficient importance that it must be retained with the paper itself. This material parallels that described under Microform Supplements but differs in that it is sufficiently important to enough readers to necessitate its inclusion in the paper.

Material prepared for publication in miniprint form should follow the guidelines of conservation of space. At present, two procedures are followed: reducing original material 50%, using the equivalent of four single-spaced manuscript pages per journal page, or reducing the material 67%, with nine one-and-one-half-spaced manuscript pages per journal page. The latter is the more common form.

Copy to be used for miniprint is submitted in camera-ready form and should be correct in nomenclature, grammatically accurate, and free. from errors. If, after the paper with accompanying miniprint material is accepted for publication, the Editorial Department notes significant discrepancies between the edited manuscript and the material submitted for miniprint, the editor will return the latter to authors for revision.

* This section does not apply to publications of the Books Department.

To prepare material that will be miniprinted, use a good ribbon and a 2-cm margin on all four sides with all typed material in the same direction of the paper. All figures, figure captions, tables, schemes, charts, structures, and equations should be similarly oriented and suitably sized. When multiple tables (or schemes, charts, etc.) are used, group them together, in numerical sequence with compatible size or design, so that one continuous flow of material is obtained.

Miniprint material (produced from author's original copy) is incorporated in the microfilm edition of the journal. It is also provided to subscribers of supplementary material (11 publications offer these subscriptions). Individual copies (microfiche; photocopy available if less than 20 pages) may also be purchased from Business Operations, Books and Journals Division.

A paragraph stating the availability of the miniprint material should be inserted at the end of the paper: "Miniprint Material Available: Experimental details for synthesis of compounds **10–15** (or similar brief description of material) (22 pages). Ordering information is given on any current masthead page."

TABLES

Tables should be used when the data therein cannot be presented clearly in the text or when more meaningful interrelationships can be conveyed. They should supplement, not duplicate, text and figures. They should be cited consecutively in the text and labeled with Roman numerals. All elements of the tables should be double spaced unless the table is submitted as camera-ready copy, in which case single space is mandatory. Each table should have a brief title. Explanatory material referring to the whole table should be included with the footnotes to the table. Table footnotes are superscript, lower case, italic letters, starting with the title footnote.

Because of composition difficulties involved in preparing tables containing structural formulas in the body of the table, when these combinations are necessary, camera-ready copy, suitable for direct photoreproduction, should be provided (*see* Figures 3 and 4). (Caution: Camera-ready copy is not edited material, nor are additions or alterations made by the Editorial Department or the printer. To ensure consistency of material in camera-ready copy with that of the rest of the manuscript, the recommendations of this handbook should be followed.) Whenever tables are submitted as camera-ready copy, they should be designed to use space effectively (single-spaced throughout) and prepared so that they are legible upon reduction (tables will be reduced to single- or double-column width; occasionally a table will be

Table III. HMO Calculations of Reduction Potentials of 1,2-Diones

Compd	M(LUMO)[a]	$E_{1/2}$ (calcd)[b]	$E_{1/2}$ (obsd)
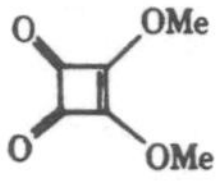 VII	0.4354	−1.88	−1.88
 III	0.3152	−1.58	
 V	0.0725	−0.99	−1.01
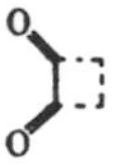 Va	−0.0757	−0.75	
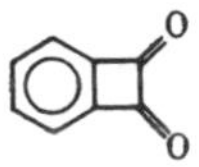 VIII	0.1567	−1.19	−1.08
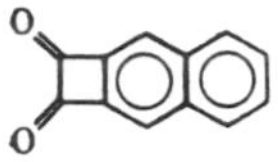 IX	0.0681	−0.97	−0.764
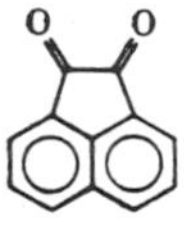 X	0.0166	−0.85	−0.828
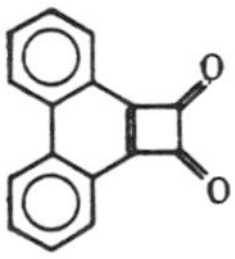 XI	0.2771	−1.48	−1.27
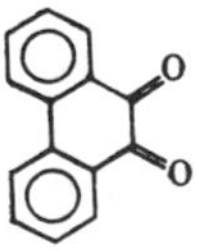 XII	−0.0980	−0.57	−0.58[c]

[a] In terms of $|\beta|$. [b] $E_{1/2} = -2.45m - 0.81$. [c] Reference 13.

Figure 3. Table consisting of structures and text. The combination presents composition difficulties; thus, the table should be submitted as camera-ready copy.

Table I. ¹H NMR Parameters of Heteroaromatic Ions[a]

Precursor	Heteroaromatic ion	

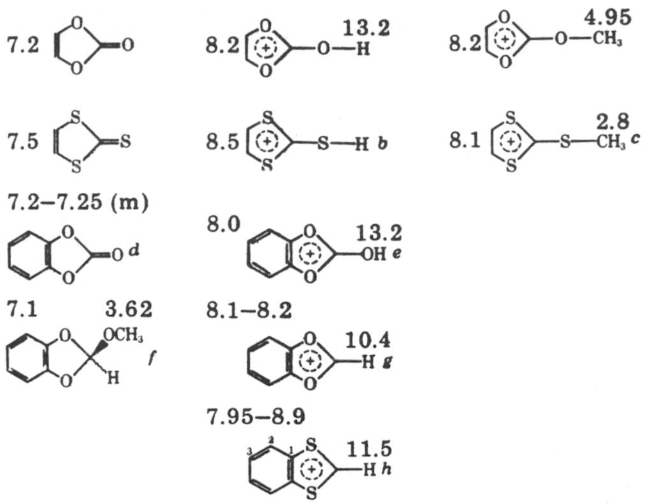

[a] In parts per million (δ) from external Me₄Si (capillary). Protonated in FSO₃H–SbF₅–SO₂ at −60 °C. Methylated with CH₃F–SbF₅ "complex"–SO₂ at −40 °C. [b] Not observable. [c] Methylated species studied as stable iodide salt in SO₂ solution at −40 °C. [d] In SO₂ClF at −10 °C. [e] Protonated in FSO₃H–SbF₅–SO₂ClF at −80 °C. [f] In CCl₄, ambient probe temperature. [g] Ion prepared in FSO₃H–SO₂ at −70 °C. [h] In CD₃CN, ambient probe temperature.

Figure 4. Table consisting primarily of structures. This presents few composition difficulties, so the requirements for submission of structures should be followed (submission of camera-ready copy is recommended).

placed parallel with the vertical alignment of the page. Whenever a judgment is made in sizing questionable material, it will generally be to greater reduction.)

Literature citations in journals (not books) that refer exclusively to tabular material and are not mentioned in the text may be given in the table footnotes. However, if the same reference is cited in more than one table, all literature citations should be collated with the reference section.

Avoid structures and equations in table footnotes (awkward constructions are generally necessary, and space is wasted). Tabular material in footnotes is also difficult to handle. All footnote material should be prepared in a linear fashion, in paragraph form.

If possible, tables in journals should occupy a single column (8.5 cm), which will take 50–75 characters and spaces. In planning the layout of tables, take into account the following considerations: relationship of size of column head to width of column, overall width of table, overall length of table (*see* discussion below).

Column Heads. Be as succinct as possible, using abbreviations and symbols whenever practical. Ideally, column heads should balance the width of the column; they should seldom be more than two lines deep. Units of measurement (SI), when applicable, should be incorporated. (Nonstandard abbreviations and symbols, when used in a table, should be defined. *See* Abbreviations, Symbols, and Units for recommendations on use of abbreviations.) Multipliers by powers of 10 are often useful because they help avoid listing values, in table columns, with an inconvenient number of digits. However, the power of 10 should follow the recommendations of ANS: "Metric Practice" (*see* p 115) and should apply to the numerical value in the quantity, not the unit. (Quantity = value × unit; e.g., temperature, symbol T, = 298 K, or time, symbol t, = 3 × 10^{-6} s. An appropriate column head for the latter example would be $t \times 10^6/$ s, $t \times 10^6$, s, $10^6 t/s$, or $10^6 t$, s, and the value in the column would be 3.)

Columns. Whenever possible, keep column widths of comparable size. In alignment of material, four practices are followed—flush left, centered, flush right, or decimal alignment. When numerical data are presented, a decimal alignment is normally followed, but the flush left alignment for text material is preferable and is easier to typeset. The Editorial Department may indicate a specific alignment for the printer to follow, but copy alignment, when satisfactory, is seldom changed. Ditto marks should not be used.

Width of Tables. Two composition processes are currently being used to produce tables in journals: photocomposition (computer-assisted) and typewriter composition (books use hot metal for nearly all composition). In photocomposition the maximum allowable width permitted is less than the vertical measure of the typical ACS journal page (25.5 cm). Tables that exceed the normal double-column spread (17.5 cm) create difficulties in photocomposition. Whenever possible, design tables so that they do not exceed this width. A problem in both composition systems involves multipart tables wherein one or more sections could occupy a single journal column, and others, double column. This creates composition difficulties, detracts from general appearance, and wastes space. Those sections narrower than others should be grouped together so that they can be "doubled-up" into two-column format.

Tables should not be interspersed in the manuscript but should be collected and placed after the reference section. However, a notation should be made in the margin to indicate where the table is first mentioned. In composition, tables are generally placed at the top of a page on or near the point of initial citation.

Short tables consisting of not more than three lines and four columns may be run directly into the text by an introductory sentence. These tables do not have titles, nor are they numbered.

Results of sequence study analyses in biochemical papers and comparison of material that requires exact vertical alignment should be submitted as camera-ready copy (*see* Figures 5–7). In addition, any table that requires special composition treatment, such as insertion of arrows or other special symbols under or over alphanumeric characters, should be submitted as camera-ready copy. (These requirements do not apply to books.)

Tables containing many data items occupy less space if they are reproduced directly from a photoreduction of a clear, typed, or computer-printed table. Use of such tables for presentation of potentio-

---

Table II: Amino Acid Sequences of Soluble Tryptic Peptides from Maleylated Histone H_{2A}.[a,b]

Tm-1	(1–3)[c]	N-Acetyl-Ser-Gly-Arg
Tm-5	(21–29)	Th Th Ala-Gly⁺Leu-Gln-Phe-Pro⁺Val-Gly-Arg
Tm-6	(30–32)	Val-His-Arg
Tm-7	(33–35)	Leu-Leu-Arg
Tm-8	(36–42)	Lys-Gly-Asn-Tyr-Ala-Glu-Arg
Tm-10	(72–77)	Asp-Asn-Lys-Lys-Thr-Arg
Tm-11	(78–81)	Ile-Ile-Pro-Arg
Tm-12	(82–88)	His-Leu-Gln-Leu-Ala-Ile-Arg
Tm-13-β	(89–99)	T Asn-Asp-Glu-Glu-Leu-Asn-Lys⁺Leu-Leu- Gly-Arg
Tm-14-β	(100–129)	Val-Thr-(Ile,Ala,Gln,Gly,Gly,Val,Leu,Pro, T Asn,Ile,Gln,Ala,Val,Leu,Leu,Pro,Lys)⁺Lys- T T Thr-Glu-Ser-His-His-Lys⁺Ala-Lys⁺Gly-Lys

[a] Methods used for determination of the sequence of peptides are indicated as follows: dansylation and Edman degradation, — and → above the amino acid residue, respectively; hydrazinolysis and carboxypeptidases A and B hydrolysis, — and ← below the amino acid residue, respectively; T and Th indicate cleavage by trypsin and thermolysin, respectively. [b] For each tryptic peptide except for peptide Tm-14-β, the arginine residue was assigned to the COOH terminus from the specificity of the trypsin limited to the arginyl bonds in a maleylated protein. The amino acid residue immediately before the arginine residue was generally placed by difference. [c] Residues.

Figure 5. Table containing special symbols and alignment and positioning requirements. These present composition difficulties and require special handling. The table should be submitted as camera-ready copy or should be redesigned as a figure.

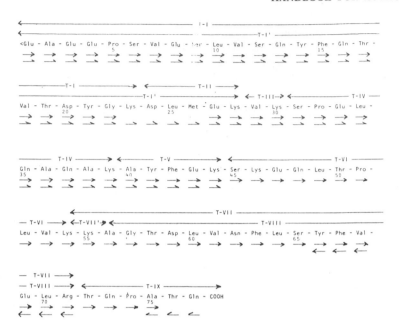

Figure 6. Material similar to that shown in Figure 4 but displayed as a figure rather than as a table. Compare the relative comprehensibility of the two.

metric data in stability constant studies, where such concise, but readable, presentation is appropriate, and for similar useful, but numerous, data is encouraged. The proportions of these tables should be such that they will fit in one- or two-column widths.

Data that may be useful to future workers but are not treated theoretically or do not form a major topic of discussion in the manuscript should not be presented in table form. Such material is often best handled by running it into the text. Examples are IR absorptions and NMR chemical shifts.

Lengthy and detailed supplementary material should be submitted for deposition as part of the Society's supplementary material program (*see* Microform Supplements).

Journal of Chemical and Engineering Data exists to publish actual data. Thus, tables are an integral part of the journal. However, special precautions should be followed for content. Entries in a table should be limited to a useful number. For example, multiple measurements can be expressed as a mean, with a statement giving deviation. If unsmoothed experimental data enhances the lasting value of the contribution, such data should be submitted. Smoothed data tables are published if they cannot be expressed as an equation and if they serve a purpose beyond that of raw data (tables of raw thermodynamic data, e.g., are usually difficult to use).

Base	Directly measured ΔG°_{300}	ΔG°_{300}	ΔH°_{300}
NH_3		0.0	0.0
i-PrOEt	0.8 1.6	0.8	1.6
$CF_3CH_2NH_2$	1.0	1.8	2.0
EtOAc	1.6	3.4	4.2
Me_2S	0.1 1.9	3.5	4.7
Et_2O	0.2 1.3 0.4	3.7	4.9
THP	0.9 0.3	4.0	5.2
THF	0.7	4.7	5.9
MeOAc	1.4 2.1	6.1	6.9
Me_2CO	1.1 1.4	7.2	8.4
MeOEt		7.5	8.3
$Me_2C{=}CH_2$	1.5 1.5 1.6	8.6	8.8
HCO_2-n-Bu	0.4 1.7	9.0	9.8
HCO_2-n-Pr	0.2 0.8	9.2	10.0
(dioxane)	1.3 1.0	9.8	11.4
HCO_2Et	0.5	10.3	11.1
i-PrCHO	0.5	10.9	11.7
n-BuCHO	0.0 0.7	10.9	11.7
Me_2O	0.1 1.6 0.8	11.0	12.2
n-PrCHO	0.7	11.8	12.6
EtCHO	1.7	13.5	14.3
HCO_2Me	0.3 1.9	13.8	14.6
MeCN	0.7 1.0 1.0	14.5	15.3

Figure 7. Table containing material difficult to reproduce accurately. Copy such as this should be submitted in camera-ready form.

The Journal of Organic Chemistry publishes registry numbers for compounds that appear in the *Chemical Abstracts* Chemical Substance, General Subject, and Formula Indexes. If data for these compounds are presented in tabular form, the registry number will often be incorporated into the table (this modification will be made by the Editorial Department). Use a column head, "registry no.", for both starting materials and products, with corresponding vacant columns. This will permit easy addition of registry numbers. (*Inorganic Chemistry* also publishes registry numbers, but the time of input is different, so no provision is made to include the numbers in tables.)

ILLUSTRATIONS

Illustrations can play a central role in understanding a paper and in pinpointing the major results. They should be included when they substantially increase comprehension; redundancy should be avoided.

Accurate, clear, and well-proportioned illustrations are important to ensure their acceptability, usefulness, and subsequent quality of reproduction. Failure of an illustration to meet the requirements usually means a publication delay.

Points that should be considered in having illustrations prepared are:

(1) Will everything be legible after reduction to single-column (or, for books, single-page) format? Space conservation is a critical factor in journal production economics; this, coupled with the fact that material demanding two or more columns may cause composition difficulties, means that most figures will be reduced to 8.5 cm or less.

(2) Are symbols and letters compatible in size? In selecting a reduction factor, the manuscript editor generally uses letters as guidelines; if these are overlarge, then too great a reduction is often requested. Conversely, when lettering in a relatively large figure is small, reduction to single column will make it almost illegible. (*See* Figures 8 and 9.)

(3) Do two (or more) figures illustrate the same feature? The figures should be combined whenever possible. This will preclude the editors' rejecting all or requiring that new figures be prepared.

(4) Are all partial figures (parts A, B, etc.) incorporated into one whole? And with optimum use of space? This will ensure compatibility in sizing, proper location, and maximum economy—the fewer pieces to process, the fewer the problems.

When submitting a manuscript containing illustrations, follow these procedures:

(1) A set of illustrations must be included with each copy of the manuscript.

(2) Original art work or glossy, positive photographic prints must be submitted with the original copy; clear reproductions may be submitted with the duplicate copies.

(3) The originals should be marked on the back with the figure number, name of the author(s), and an abbreviated title of the article

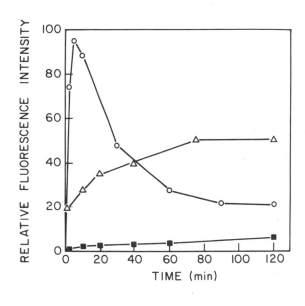

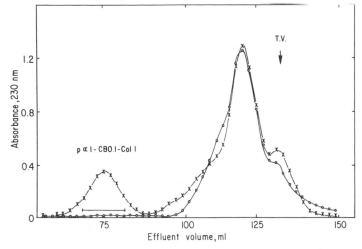

Figure 8. (*above*) Illustration in which symbols and letters are proportionately sized. (*below*) Illustration in which symbols are disproportionately smaller than letters.

Width of drawing	*Minimum height for:*			*Thickness of ruled lines*
To fit single text column in journal: 17 cm	Lower case letters	Numerals & capital letters	Symbols within drawings	Light, #1 Leroy _____ for graph grids, bonds, arrows
To fit double text column in journal: 36 cm	3 mm	4 mm	3 mm	Medium, #2 Leroy ▬▬▬▬ for graph borders or reference lines
				Heavy, #5 Leroy ▬▬▬▬ for graph curves or emphasis lines

Figure 9. Standard sizes for lines and lettering to be used in the drafting of original illustrations. Material drawn to these specifications will be reduced to one-half original size and will fit satisfactorily into the column widths.

for efficient identification during handling by the editors and printer.

(4) Art work offered for reproduction should never be folded.

(5) Whenever practical, original illustrations should be drawn on 22 × 28 cm sheets for handling convenience. A clear space of at least 2.5 cm around the illustration is needed for markings, identification, and handling.

(6) All illustrations should be numbered in sequence, with Arabic numerals, in order of appearance in the text. Number as Figure 1, Figure 2, etc. Avoid terms such as "Chart" or "Plate". (Chart is reserved for displays of structural formulas; plate generally refers to material that requires special processing, with concomitant additional expense. Authors are expected to defray the costs.)

(7) Every figure must have a caption that includes the figure number and a brief, informative title. If more information is needed, use complete sentences and standard punctuation. If possible, the caption should provide enough detail to make the figure self-contained.

(8) Symbols should be simple (○, ●, □, ■, △, ▲, for example); do not use unusual shapes or superpositions.

(9) Keys to symbols and other data should appear in the caption, not in the figure itself, unless the symbols are complex and cannot be easily composed.

(10) Avoid using dashed lines, with the dashes of unequal length, to differentiate among curves (it is difficult to duplicate the distinction in figure captions).

(11) During the publication cycle, figures and captions may be processed separately. All figure captions, therefore, should by typed together, double-spaced, on a separate page(s).

(12) No figures should be incorporated with the text.

Photographs. To obtain satisfactory half-tone reproductions, high-contrast, glossy, black-and-white continuous tone prints are most desirable. (A screen, if used, should not exceed 133 lines; a 120-line screen is recommended.)

(1) Photographs should be mailed flat, well protected by heavy cardboard.

(2) Do not punch holes in photographs or fasten them with metal clips. The emulsion surface must be free of irregularities and markings.

(3) Each print should be clearly labeled on the back as indicated above; when doubt could arise, indicate which edge is the top of the illustration.

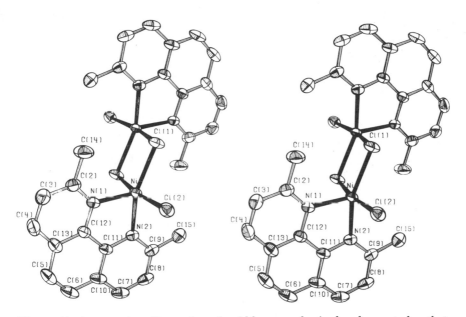

Figure 10. A stereoview. Stereoviews should be properly sized and mounted so that they can be used without further modification.

Stereoviews. Stereo diagrams must be submitted properly mounted so that they can be reproduced in full size (100%) or using a simple reduction factor of 2 (50%), 3 (33%), or 4 (25%). Thus the distance between similar points on the original should be between 5.5 and 6.4 cm (100%), ~11 cm (for 50% reduction), ~17 cm (for reduction to 33%), or ~22 cm (25%) (*see* Figure 10).

Color Presentations. If use of color would enhance presentation, and if the author defrays the considerable additional expense involved in production, both two-color and four-color processes are available. For the former, prepare two diagrams, one to be printed with black ink, the second, in color. When superimposed, the two should form a harmonious composite.

For four-color work, a color separation must be made. A large color transparency or a 35-mm negative will generally result in a satisfactory reproduction. Consult the Editorial Department for further information on procedures and recommendations.

Drawings and Graphs. Uniformity should be maintained in all art work prepared for a single manuscript. Freehand or typewritten lettering should not be used. Note the recommendations in this handbook for symbols and abbreviations to be used on diagrams. The suggestions that follow are guides to the preparation of drawings that can be reproduced in journals.

(1) A good illustration is clear and simple; keep lines and wording to a minimum.

(2) Avoid showing more than four or five curves on one illustration (*see* Figure 11).

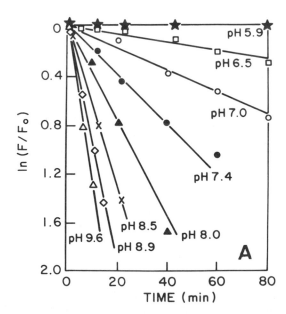

Figure 11. A well-designed figure (symbols and letters are compatibly sized; symbols are easily distinguished from each other and can be easily identified in the caption) that loses some impact because of too much information. This alternative is preferred, however, to that of using two separate figures to convey the same amount of information.

(3) Avoid interlaced or unrelated curves.

(4) Keep the figure as compact as possible (avoid wasted white space).

(5) If possible, design illustrations for printing to fit the width of one journal column, usually about 8.5 cm. (Greater latitude exists for books.) The original drawing should be twice the publication size, that is, 17 cm. The height of the drawing will vary to meet individual requirements. Reproduced illustrations wider than column width should fit within the overall width of the text on the journal page, usually about 17.5 cm.

(6) If figures are divided into parts, all parts must be combined on one 22 × 28 composite, with minimum spacing (4 mm) between individual segments. All pieces should be compatibly sized and esthetically assembled, with a minimum of space used.

Drafting Instructions—In preparing the final copy use one of the following (in order of preference):

(1) 32 lb white ledger paper, 100% rag content (suitable for ink work);

(2) three-ply Bristol board (such as Strathmore or equivalent);

(3) tracing cloth or vellum.

Commercial graph paper is not recommended. However, paper printed in a nonphotographic blue may be used if the significant coordinate lines are overruled in black ink.

Use black India drawing ink. Lead pencil should not be used. A light nonphotographic blue pencil should be used for guide lines not to be reproduced.

Follow the recommendations in Figure 9 for standard lettering and lines. Use mechanical lettering sets, such as Leroy, Wrico, or equivalent. They provide uniform lettering of the right degree of boldness. Dry transfer lettering (pressure or rub-on lettering) is also recommended; it is available in print of different sizes. These letters and symbols are quick and easy to use and facilitate consistency and neatness. *Do not use a typewriter to letter illustrations.* The normal size of lettering for the printed page in journals is considered to be 4.5 points high (ignoring ascenders or descenders), 6 points high in books. This is approximately equal to 2 mm. Thus, letters and symbols in original drawings to be reduced by one-half should be 4 mm. The original size of letters should not exceed 6 mm or the letters will be too large in relationship to the body of the drawing.

To improve the visual appearance of line graphs observe the following additional suggestions:

(1) A ruled open grid must be used if quantitative reference to the figure is to be made. Tick marks may be used if only semiquantitative presentation is desired.

(2) The grid scale for each axis should be chosen thoughtfully with full understanding of how the choice of grid proportion affects the plotted curves. A well-designed grid has proportions that show the picture properly and the number and kind of rulings that help the reader to understand the character of the data and to read the curve with the desired exactness.

(3) Show all scale numbers and titles outside the grid border.

(4) The axes must be labeled clearly with both the quantity measured and the units in which it is measured (all abbreviations and symbols should conform to those recommended in this handbook).

(5) Each label should be parallel to its axis.

(6) All lettering and numbers should read from left to right if possible or from bottom to top if necessary.

(7) For plot points, use template data symbols. Avoid small, freehand marks. Height of symbols should not exceed 4 mm; the height should be the same as that of lower case letters. (Size of symbol is often varied to indicate error in any given value; if this is done, the smallest symbol should not be smaller than 2.5 mm.)

The following symbols are recommended in the order of preference:

●, ▲, ■, ○, △, □, ◐, ◑, ◓, ◒, ◊, ♦, ×, +

(8) The journal or book requirements for style should be followed (the manuscript will be edited in accord with the recommendations of this handbook; if the figures differ in style from the manuscript, no modifications will be made by the editorial staff, nor will substitutions be made after the original figure is processed).

STRUCTURAL FORMULAS

Structural formulas are an integral part of many papers published in American Chemical Society publications. Their importance in transmitting information in a conceptual fashion cannot be overemphasized. For this reason accurate representation and design are extremely important.

Camera-ready copy, prepared with the space requirements of the publication in mind and with all component parts (label information) intact, should be submitted with the original manuscript. Freehand drawing is unacceptable. Templates and stencils should be used. A Rapidograph pen, point No. 0, is recommended for drawing bonds, arrows, benzene rings, and the many variations of geometrical designs which are encountered in structures. Special attention should be given to correctness of symbols, to locations of subscripts, superscripts, and ionic charges, and to the placing and joining of bond lines.

Stencilling sets for preparing diagrams and instruction books describing their use can be obtained from Verlag Chemie ("Instructions for the use of the stencil for drawing organic structural formulas", and "Formula Stencil II. Stereochemistry", Verlag Chemie International, Inc., 175 Fifth Avenue, New York, NY 10010, 1975) and Alpha/Ventron ("Seyferth" stencil; 152 Andover St., Danvers, MA 01923).

Structural formulas should be prepared with care and also with a view to the most economical use of space. All structures should be numbered consecutively from left to right, top to bottom, in boldface Arabic numerals, regardless of the order in which the compounds occur in the text. Repetition of the same structure should be avoided; the number of an earlier structure may be used alone if a compound occurs several times. Compounds with similar structure should be indicated by modification of a parent structure. Use a general designation, X, for the point of difference; then, e.g.,

$$\textbf{13}, X = Cl$$
$$\textbf{14}, X = Br$$
$$\textbf{15}, X = OCH_3$$

Arrange structural formulas in horizontal rows so that the display or block will fill a single-column width or, for very large groups, an entire page width. If this is not done, it may be necessary to rearrange the display, with possible loss of clarity, to avoid waste of space on the journal page. The following points will help the author adjust formula layouts to the correct sizes.

(1) A single column width will accommodate 13 contiguous six-membered rings or an equivalent amount of linear structures.

(2) Three letters (in a side chain or above an arrow) are approximately equivalent to one ring.

(3) A bond line to a side chain is half the width of a ring.

(4) Subscript numbers require half a letter width.

(5) For clarity, a space equivalent to one bond line should be left between formulas.

(6) Symbols on arrows between formulas should be as brief and compact as possible. Abbreviations such as Me for CH_3, Et for C_2H_5, Ph (not ϕ) for C_6H_5, and partial structures are useful for saving space (see Abbreviations, Symbols, and Units and Figure 12).

If a 12-mm ring size in the drawings and the allowances given for lettering, side chains, and spaces are used, the material in a 17.5-cm-wide column (normal typed page) in the manuscript will fit into one column on the printed page. This ring size is No. 16 on the Rapidesign No. 50 Pocket Pal template or No. 11 on the Fieser Chemist's Triangle.

If it is necessary to arrange structures for a full-page width, a 36-cm width drawing is possible with 12-mm rings. If a satisfactory arrangement is slightly larger than the limits for a one-column presentation, it is preferable to stagger or overlap structures in successive rows rather than spread out the display to a full page width. In multiring structures such as steroids, partial structures showing only the pertinent points are encouraged. For examples of finished formula layouts, *see* the discussion on preparation of figures.

In structural layouts involving odd-shaped rings, bicyclic structures, etc., the shapes of these structures should be consistent throughout. In

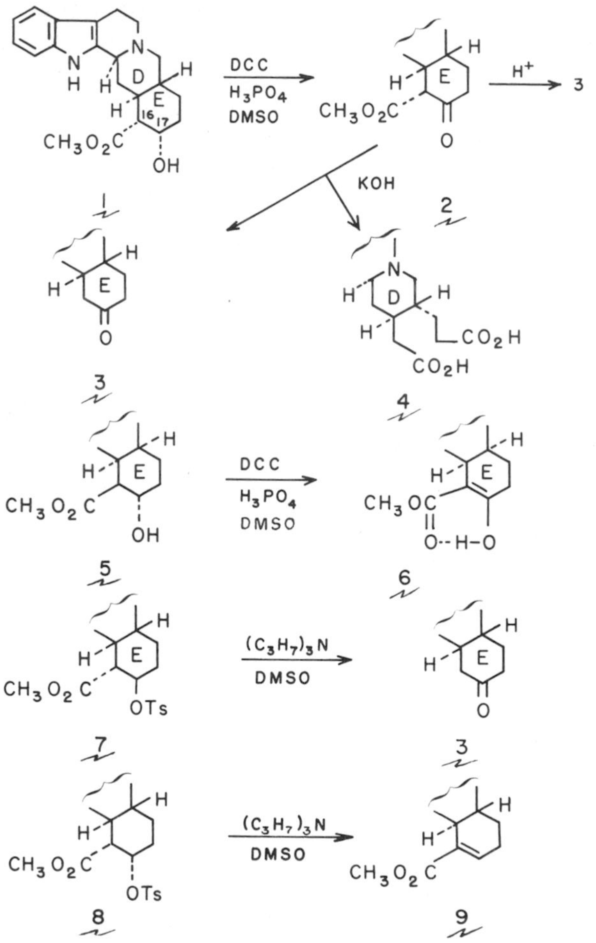

Figure 12. Reaction diagram using space to good advantage (note partial structures). However, when material is used as camera-ready copy, the wavy line under the compound numbers will be reproduced. (Camera-ready copy will not be retouched to eliminate extraneous marks.)

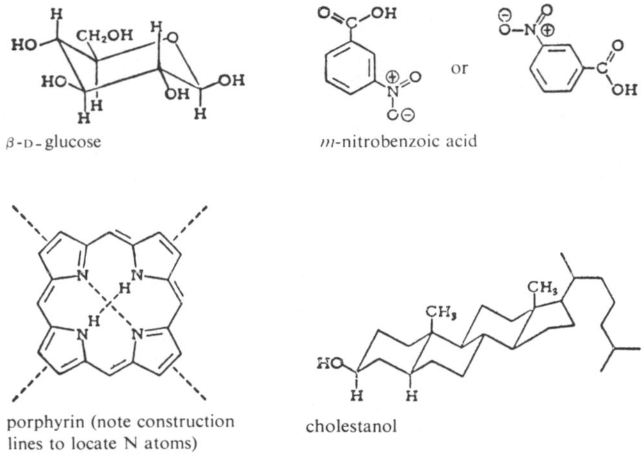

β-D-glucose   m-nitrobenzoic acid

porphyrin (note construction   cholestanol
lines to locate N atoms)

Figure 13. Structures drawn with the aid of the Fieser Chemist's Triangle template. The label data have been inserted by typewriter, so that the overall effect is not graphic arts quality.

preparing camera-ready copy of complex drawings, the same general points and requirements for lettering size apply that are discussed for illustrations (*see* Figure 13).

In drawing structural formulas the author should strive to reach the best possible representation of molecular geometry. In three-dimensional drawings of chemical structures, the lines in the background that are crossed by lines in the foreground should be broken to give a greater three-dimensional effect. Also, lines in the foreground can be made heavier.

Do not use structures when they are unnecessary (C_6H_6 is a perfectly adequate representation of benzene, and ClC_6H_5 or $1,4-Cl_2C_6H_4$ are both meaningful forms). Do not supply art for material that can and should be portrayed on one line. Do not supply art for any linear formula that will be used alone. Do not make angular a formula that could be portrayed linearly unless the spatial relationship must be portrayed.

Structures in tables present special composition difficulties. If their use is absolutely necessary, and if the structures are part of the table columns, then the entire table should be prepared for photoreduction (*see* Tables). If a structure is part of the table title or applicable to all column heads, art for that segment only should be provided. Under no circumstances will art be added to the body of a table that is expected to be composed by the printer.

When equation numbers are used, they should be Arabic numbers, light face, in parentheses at the right-hand margin in the text. Sequential numbering of all equations, mathematical or chemical, should be maintained. Do not confuse equation numbers with compound numbers, which are set in boldface type.

All American Chemical Society journals and some of its books are produced by computer-assisted photocomposition. With advancing technology, more segments of a manuscript can be incorporated into a total system. At the time of printing of this handbook complicated structural arrays cannot be produced economically and esthetically by the composition system; they must be manually drafted. However, the time is near when schemes and charts will be effectively presented as an integral part of the photocomposition output. At such time, the requirement for providing art with manuscript copy will be relaxed or eliminated. The instructions to authors of individual journals will be modified to reflect this change when it is applicable. Accurate presentation will still be necessary, however, to ensure effective and accurate output, so the recommendations outlined in this section, with the exception of the "finished" nature of the product, will remain valid.

FORMAT FOR DOCUMENTATION

Footnotes. There are two kinds of footnotes, those of content and those of reference.

Content footnotes provide a place for material that the writer wishes to include in his report but which would disrupt the flow of thought if introduced into the text. They are used to amplify or to qualify textual discussion and to make acknowledgments. Most journals discourage the use of content footnotes except as noted below; they are not permitted in books.

Reference footnotes are used in some journals to cite the authority for statements in the text. These footnotes are also used for cross-references to other parts of the work.

Content footnotes should be used to indicate the address of the corresponding author when the address differs from that given in the contribution line. In almost all other instances, information that might be suitable for a footnote should instead be incorporated into the text, enclosed within parentheses, at the point where the explanation is warranted, or cited in proper numerical order and listed in the references and notes section.

Accounts of Chemical Research retains a format that lists references and notes at the bottom of columns in which those citations occur. In a format such as this, it is imperative that content footnotes be numbered consecutively with reference footnotes.

In *Biochemistry* it is customary to give contribution and receipt information, acknowledgments of support, current addresses, and information on abbreviations as footnotes. These will always be on the first page of the article, and their citation should be indicated by pertinent symbols (†, ‡, §, ¶) after the title or in the byline. Other footnotes should be avoided.

Explanatory material for tables should be given as footnotes to the table. Schemes and charts may also require footnotes. In figures, such information should be incorporated in the captions.

References. The "American National Standard for Bibliographic References", ANSI Z39.29-1977, has recently been completed. It provides rules and guidelines for preparing bibliographic references. The standard encompasses a variety of items, but for each it indicates essential, recommended, and optional elements. In addition, the standard provides for consistency in format but does permit certain options. The preferred order of groups of information within a standard reference is: author, title, edition, imprint, physical description, series statement, and notes. Among the options listed in the standard is the location of the date of publication (part of the imprint group).

References in American Chemical Society books and journals adhere to ANSI Z39.29-1977 recommendations by requiring all references to include the essential elements of a bibliographic citation. In addition, some of the elements recommended by ANSI are required in our reference formats. Options exercised are location of date and font selection. Punctuation is an occasional point of divergence from the standard. (The ANSI recommendations consider a reference to consist of a series of elements. Each element has the weight of a sentence, and its termination is signaled by a period. Internal construction of each element is also heavily punctuated with colons and semicolons. Many references in American Chemical Society publications are interspersed with notes. The multisentence form of a single reference, combined with the normal sentence structure of a note, would yield an unwieldy mix.) Authors may follow the ANSI recommendations regarding punctuation; modifying to specific book or journal style is a simple editorial conversion.

The author is responsible for the accuracy and completeness of all references in his paper. All parts of a reference listing should be checked against the original document. A reference must include certain minimum data, as follows: journals—author, abbreviated journal title, year of publication, volume number, initial page of cited article; books—

author, book title, publisher, city of publication, year of publication. For citations of material other than books and journals enough information must be provided so that the material can be identified and located. Publications such as company records that are not considered part of the permanent literature should not be included in the list of references.

A. References to Journals

In references, journal titles should be abbreviated based on the rules in International Organization for Standardization, "Documentation—International code for the abbreviation of titles of periodicals" (ISO 4-1972(E)) and title word abbreviations found in International Organization for Standardization, "Documentation—International list of periodical title word abbreviations" (ISO 833-1974(E)). Since ISO 4 allows options, those selected by the Chemical Abstracts Service should be followed. "Chemical Abstracts Service Source Index" (*CASSI*) and its quarterly supplements provide a complete list of recommended journal abbreviations, as well as detailed and accurate bibliographic data. "Bibliographic Guide for Editors & Authors", published by BIOSIS/CAS/Ei, is also a valuable reference, especially for the approved abbreviated titles of periodicals.

There are two general treatments of reference citations within American Chemical Society journals: that in which the reference is cited by number in the text and that in which the reference is cited by author(s) name and date.

Accounts of Chemical Research, Advances in Chemistry Series, ACS Symposium Series, Analytical Chemistry, Chemical Reviews, Environmental Science & Technology, Inorganic Chemistry, Journal of the American Chemical Society, Journal of Chemical and Engineering Data, Journal of Chemical Information and Computer Sciences, Journal of Medicinal Chemistry, The Journal of Organic Chemistry, The Journal of Physical Chemistry, and *Macromolecules* use numerical reference citations.

Biochemistry, Industrial & Engineering Chemistry Fundamentals, Industrial & Engineering Chemistry Process Design and Development, Industrial & Engineering Chemistry Product Research and Development, and *Journal of Agricultural and Food Chemistry* cite references in the text as follows: (Adams, 1972; Brooks and Green, 1974a,c; Brooks et al., 1975).

With numerical reference citations, start with 1 and number consecutively throughout the paper. If a reference is repeated, do not give it a new number; use the original reference number. When more than one reference is cited at one point, separate the numbers by commas, or if they are part of a consecutive series, use a dash (1, 3, 5–7, 10). These citations should be given (a) as superscript numbers, without parentheses and without spaces, for *Accounts of Chemical Research, Chemical Reviews, Inorganic Chemistry, Journal of the American Chemical Society, Journal of Chemical Information and Computer Sciences, The Journal of Organic Chemistry, The Journal of Physical Chemistry,* and *Macromolecules*; (b) as italic numbers, on the line, in parentheses, for *ACS Symposia Series, Advances in Chemistry Series, Analytical Chemistry, Environmental Science & Technology,* and *Journal of Chemical and Engineering Data.*

When citation is by author name and date, avoid needless repetition and duplication. For example: Smith and Jones, 1969a; Green, 1972; Ward, 1973; Smith and Jones, 1972; Green, 1975 could be condensed into three entries: Smith and Jones, 1969a, 1972; Green, 1972, 1975; Ward, 1973. Note: with more than two authors, et al. is used.

All references should be collated at the end of the manuscript: in numerical order if cited by number and in alphabetical order if cited by author.

Below are examples of bibliographic references most frequently used as they should appear in the typed manuscript.* The information that must be supplied, the order of appearance for each item, and points of style, such as font selection, punctuation, and capitalization, are indicated. Recent issues of the publications should be consulted for individual style preferences. (Many of the style changes in this handbook were initiated in 1977; however, reference citations in journals prior to 1978 differ from these recommendations, and 1978 citation formats have not been changed to conform to these recommendations.)

(1) Schulman, J. M.; Venanzi, Thomas. *J. Am. Chem. Soc.* **1976,** *98,* 4701–6.

(2) Winston, A.; Wichacheewa, P. *Macromolecules* **1973,** *6,* 200.

Bowers, M. T.; Chau, M. *J. Phys. Chem.* **1976,** *80,* 1739–42.

Cherry, R. J.; Cogoli, A.; Opplizer, M.; Schneider, G.; Gemenza, G. *Biochemistry* **1976,** *15,* 3653.

Note that full author names are acceptable, but not mandatory. Inclusive pagination is encouraged. Indentation (paragraph or reverse) is a matter of book or journal style.

Type font is often varied from element to element in these citations. Journal title is italicized in American Chemical Society publications. Do not mark the manuscript for font unless you are certain of the correctness of your instructions.

---

* Refer to the Instructions to Authors, *Biochemistry* **1978,** *17*(1), for citation format in *Biochemistry.*

References to journals that begin every issue with page one should include the issue number in parentheses following the volume number.

(3) Doe, A. B. *Chem. Eng. News* **1966,** *44*(41), 23.

When reference is made to an abstract of an article, this should be indicated. If possible, references to both the original article and the abstract should be given.

(4) Roe, C. D. *Zh. Fiz. Khim.* **1963,** *50,* 1234; *Chem. Abstr.* **1963,** *56,* 112*a*.

References to the English translation of articles printed in a non-English-language journal should, if possible, also include reference to the original article.

(5) Doe, A. B. *J. Gen. Chem. USSR (Engl. Transl.)* **1960,** *30,* 2050; *Zh. Obshch. Khim.* **1960,** *30,* 2100.

Some serial publications appear in hard cover form (The *Enzymes,* many Advances, Progress, Annual Reviews). Since these are serial publications and they are listed in *CASSI,* they should be treated as journals.

B. References to Books

In addition to authors, title, and year of publication, minimum essential information required for books includes place of publication and publisher. Editor, volume number, chapter, and page number should be included when relevant.

Woodburn, John H. "Taking Things Apart and Putting Things Together"; American Chemical Society: Washington, D.C., 1976; p 68.

(6) Vanderbilt, B. M. "Thomas Edison, Chemist"; American Chemical Society: Washington, D.C., 1971.

(7) Cross, A. D.; Jones, R. A. "Introduction to Practical Infra-Red Spectroscopy", 3rd ed.; Plenum: New York, 1969; Chapter 2.

For instances in which reference is not to the author or editor of a whole book, but to a contributor to a part of it, the reference should be written as follows:

(8) Smith, A. B. In "Fluorine Chemistry", 4th ed.; Doe, J. S., Ed.; Jones: New York, 1964; Vol. I, Chapter 7.

C. References to Special Materials

Theses

(9) Doe, L. A. Ph.D. Dissertation, The State University, New York, N.Y., 1963.

Government Bulletins

(10) "Selected Values of Chemical and Thermodynamic Properties". *Natl. Bur. Stand. (U.S.) Circ.* **1950,** No. 500.

Reports

(11) Roe, L.; Doe, J. R. Los Altos, Calif., Feb 1964, AEC Report 66-170.

Patents

(12) Doe, A. B. U.S. Patent 2 542 356, 1952.
(13) Roed, R. U.S. Patent 3 000 000, 1960; *Chem. Abstr.* **1961,** *51,* 2870.
(14) Doe, A. B. British Patent 1 034 050, 1966.

Abstracts of Meeting Papers

(15) Roe, N.; Doe, D. "Abstracts of Papers", 172nd National Meeting of the American Chemical Society, San Francisco, Calif., Aug 1976; American Chemical Society: Washington, D.C., 1976; INOR 53.
(16) Doe, N. Centennial Meeting of the American Chemical Society, New York, N.Y., April 1976; American Chemical Society: Washington, D.C.; Abstr. CELL 67.

D. References to Unpublished Materials

For material presented before a society or other organization, but not published, use the following form:

(17) Roe, A. B., presented in part at the XXth Congress of the International Union of Chemistry, Paris, Sept 1960.

For material accepted for publication but not yet published, use the following form:

(18) Roe, A. B. *Spectrochim. Acta,* in press.

volume number, page number, and year should be added if they are available by the time the author receives the galley proofs.

For material submitted for publication but not yet accepted, use the following form (except for *Biochemistry,* in which entries such as these should not be in literature citations):

(19) Roe, A. B., submitted for publication in *Spectrochim. Acta.*

Books cite submitted items as unpublished data.

For personal communications, name of the writer, affiliation, and date should be given (in *Biochemistry,* this information should be incorporated into the text):

(20) Doe, C. D., The State University, personal communication, 1963.

In citation of personal communications the author should obtain permission from the person to be quoted.

In *Biochemistry, Environmental Science & Technology, Industrial & Engineering Chemistry Fundamentals, Industrial & Engineering Chemistry Process Design and Development, Industrial & Engineering Chemistry Product Research and Development, Journal of Agricultural and Food Chemistry,* and *Journal of Chemical Information and Computer Sciences,* unpublished work (unless already accepted for publication) and personal communications may be included in the list of references or may be cited within the text as follows (in *Biochemistry* they must be cited as follows; in books, they should be included in the literature cited): (A. B. Roe and G. Doe, 1972, unpublished data); (A. B. Roe, 1975, personal communication).

Permission to Reprint

Whenever a manuscript contains material (tables, figures, charts, schemes, etc.) that appeared in a medium that is copyright to a person or organization other than the American Chemical Society, the permission of the copyright holder to reprint the material is necessary. It is the obligation of the author to secure this permission. In addition, if the copyright material is from papers of other authors (rather than the author(s) who is submitting the manuscript in question), prior approval of that author should also be obtained.

A typical acknowledgment should read: Reprinted with permission from ref 32 [or Reprinted with permission from Smith and Jones (1976)]. Copyright 1976 American Institute of Physics.

Miscellaneous

This handbook considers many of the problems encountered in papers submitted to the Society for publication. However, questions on format and arrangement that are not covered in this handbook may arise in manuscript preparation. When such is the case, follow the recommendations in the instructions to authors of a journal and/or consult recent issues for format. In addition, other handbooks may be useful. In mathematics, consult "A Manual for Authors of Mathematical Papers" (American Mathematical Society); in physics, "Style Manual" (American Institute of Physics); in biology, "CBE Style Manual" (Council of Biology Editors).

Submission of Final Copy

Manuscripts submitted to the books and journals must be in a form suitable for publication. The editorial staff will not make extensive changes in areas which do not conform to publication style. Manuscripts that do not follow the publication's conventions and requirements may be returned to the authors with a request that the authors revise the paper to conform with accepted style and practice.

TYPING

Manuscripts must be typewritten double-spaced, on one side only, on 22 × 28 cm, heavy-duty, white bond paper. Three good copies should be submitted. A set of illustrations must accompany each copy: one set of ink tracings or glossy prints with the ribbon copy and two sets of photocopied illustrations.

Double space all copy: references, footnotes, tables, abstract, and figure captions as well as regular text. A liberal margin, 2 cm, should be left on all sides of each page. (Special instructions are necessary for material that will be used in microform only; *see* pertinent directions under Microform Supplements and Miniprint Material and in Appendix F.)

For instructions on preparing various portions of the manuscript, *see* the recommendations in Sections II and III of this handbook. Additional hints to the typist are included in Appendix G.

The final copy should be as nearly letter perfect as possible. If a correction must be made, cross out the error and type the correct version above it. The use of correction tape or correction fluid to obliterate some errors is also recommended. Overtyping an incorrect letter with a correct letter gives the printer no indication of which letter to print. Do not type in margins or below the lines, or attach slips of paper to the pages. Retype any page needing lengthy insertions. Extensive handwritten revisions are not acceptable.

Handwritten directions covering specific points (identification of special characters, e.g.) should be made in the margin. The notation "use throughout" will aid both editor and printer.

ARRANGEMENT

The title page should include the title, byline, and author's affiliation (except in those journal types, such as communications in *Journal of the American Chemical Society,* that place byline and author affiliation at the end of the manuscript; in all instances, follow journal practice). The abstract should be on a separate page (if the abstract is to be printed, this page should be numbered; if the abstract is exclusively for transmittal to *Chemical Abstracts,* this page should not be numbered, but should be identified by title and author(s) names). All pages of a manuscript should be numbered consecutively, including the title page and list of footnotes and/or references (except the page containing the abstract when that abstract will not be published). Page numbers should appear at top right. If a page is inserted or removed after the final copy has been prepared, succeeding page numbers must be altered accordingly. References, tables, captions, and figures should be placed in that order, at the end of the paper. The captions should be grouped on one or more separate pages.

MAILING

All manuscripts should be sent by first-class mail to the Editor or Managing Editor at the address given in the masthead of the appropriate journal. Illustrations including glossy prints and photographs should be adequately protected with cardboard.

A brief letter of transmittal should accompany each manuscript. The letter should contain a clear statement of intent that the manuscript be considered for publication, the name of the author, the title of the manuscript, and the complete address (the zip code must be included in U.S. addresses) to which the proofs should be sent. Membership in the American Chemical Society is not a prerequisite for publication in its books and journals.

In general it is not necessary to include explanatory notes telling why that specific journal was chosen or discussing the manuscript. Submission of a manuscript to one of the Society journals means that the same work is not under consideration for publication elsewhere, and that, if accepted, it will not be published elsewhere without the consent of the Society (*see also* Liability and Copying Rights, p 88).

Receipt of each manuscript will be acknowledged.

IV. THE EDITORIAL PROCESS

Manuscript Review

Papers submitted to journals of the American Chemical Society are considered for publication with the understanding that they have not been published or accepted for publication elsewhere and are not currently under consideration elsewhere.

The following consensus statement of American Chemical Society editors represents current peer-review practices of American Chemical Society journals and books:

"Manuscripts submitted for publication in ACS research journals and in certain ACS book series, after screening by editors for scope appropriate to the intended publication, are generally reviewed by two or more individuals. Reviewers are chosen on the basis of their known expertise in the research field covered by the manuscript. The ability of an individual to render an objective, critical review is also considered in reviewer selection.

"Among the criteria reviewers are asked to use in judging manuscripts are: originality of the work, its significance to the research field, the validity of experimental data, the adequacy of supporting information, and the soundness and logic of interpretation. The specific criteria used vary according to the particular editorial requirements of each journal or book.

"Authors are sent pertinent reviewer comments by the Editor, generally with the identity of a reviewer removed. The final decision to publish is the responsibility of the Editor. Although decisions are nearly always based on reviewers' comments, each Editor retains the right to publish in the face of negative comments and to reject in the face of positive comments. In practice, however, editorial decisions that run contrary to reviewer recommendations are usually related to journal or book scope or involve manuscripts in the Editor's particular field of expertise."

A paper that is rejected may be reconsidered if the author presents a good case for further review.

After a paper is accepted, it is considered to be in final form. Alterations made subsequent to acceptance may be permitted subject to editorial discretion. If alterations are extensive or if significant additions are made, additional review may be required.

Processing of Accepted Manuscripts

All accepted manuscripts for journals go directly from the editor or managing editor to the Editorial Department, where they are prepared for the printer. The person submitting the manuscripts is notified of acceptance by the editor. Comparable processing is followed by the Books Department.

TECHNICAL EDITING

The technical editing of papers submitted to books and journals of the American Chemical Society is quite extensive. In addition to the routine matters of giving instructions to the printer, marking the copy according to publication style, selection of type, preparation of layout, etc., the editing staff attempts to ensure consistency, clarity, and grammatical accuracy, introduces changes to improve nomenclature, graphics presentation, tabular format, etc., and initiates dialogues with editors and/or authors to clarify material or to expedite processing. The staff tries to achieve an accurate and timely publication that is as esthetic as the composition system permits with the material at hand.

AUTHOR'S PROOF

One author, generally the author to whom correspondence should be addressed, receives a copy of the manuscript set in type—"galley" proof—for final approval before publication. A manuscript generally cannot be released for printing until the author's proof has been returned to the Editorial or the Books Department. Hence, proof should be checked and mailed back promptly according to individual journal or book instructions. To save time and reduce expense, foreign contributors may authorize a colleague in the United States to correct proof.

Proof should be checked thoroughly. When checking, the author should read it carefully, at least two times (one of which should be done against the manuscript). Only corrections and necessary changes should be made. Extensive changes may require editorial approval, require a new date of receipt, and delay publication. Printer's errors are corrected at no cost to the authors, but authors may be charged the cost of extensive resetting made necessary by their own alterations.

Data obtained after original submission of the manuscript should not be added to the text, but may be attached to the galley proofs. A copy of the new information must be forwarded to the editor with an explanatory note. Where the desirability or necessity for the inclusion of such material can be demonstrated to the satisfaction of the editors, it will be inserted as a Note Added in Proof. (In books, galleys are amended when possible.)

In marking the galley proofs observe the following points:

(1) Check all text, data, references against the original manuscript.

(2) Mark corrections in the margins of the galley proof in pencil (ink is used by editors and printers).

(3) Do not erase or in any way wholly obliterate type in the text. Instead, strike one line through the copy to be deleted, extend the line to the margin, and insert the indicated change.

(4) Pay particular attention to equations, formulas, tables, captions, spelling of proper names, and numbering of illustrations, tables, and references.

(5) Clarify complicated corrections by rewriting the entire phrase or sentence in the margin and encircle to indicate to the compositor that it is not an addition.

(6) Answer explicitly all queries made by the technical editor.

Proofreader's Marks. Every correction must be indicated in the margin; therefore each one requires two marks, one within the printed material and one in the margin. The one within the printed page is usually a caret or a line indicating where the correction is to be made. Marks to be used in correcting proofs are listed in Table IV. Do *not* make unnecessary or superfluous changes (e.g., do not strike out an entire word, and insert the plural of that word; an "s" in the margin generally suffices).

Table IV: Proofreaders' Marks			
mark in margin	mark in proof	example	meaning
Size and Style of Type			
wf, α	circle character	In the ⊚-helical conformation . .	wrong font (size or style of type)
lc	/ through letter	The x-ray diffraction . . .	set in lower case

Table IV (Continued)

mark in margin	mark in proof	example	meaning
caps	triple underscore	An erlenmeyer flask was . . .	set in capitals
sc	double underscore	the addition of d-glucose . . .	set in small caps
ital	single underscore	cis-1,3-dimeth- ylcyclohexane . .	set in italic (or oblique) type
rom	circle character	with triphenyl- methane react . .	set in roman type
bf	wavy line	Experimental Section	set in boldface type
lf	circle character	compound (III) . .	set in lightface type
-1	insert ∨	near 3500 cm-1 .	superior letter or figure
a	insert ∧	calculation of the pKa . . .	inferior letter or figure

Punctuation

⊙	at point of insertion or through punctuation to be changed, insert ∧	be used. The . .	insert or substi- tute period
⌢	∧ or /, as above	books/ jour- nals, and . . .	insert or substi- tute comma
:	∧ or /, as above	payable to/ American Chem-. .	insert or substi- tute colon
;	∧ or /, as above	column width, how- ever . . . ∧	insert or substi- tute semicolon
᾿	∧ or circle character to be changed	the Societys publications . .	insert or substi- tute apostrophe

Table IV (Continued)

mark in margin	mark in proof	example	meaning
⌄|	∧ or circle character to be changed	the pKa∧	insert or substitute prime
‶ ‷	∧ or circle as above	a ∧Guide for Authors∧ . . .	insert or substitute quotations
=	∧ or circle as above	the 3∧g sam-ple . . .	insert or substitute hyphen
= (equals)	∧ or circle as above	x ⊕ a . . .	insert or substitute equal sign
c=c (double bond)	∧ or circle as above	CH_2 ⊜ CH . .	insert or substitute double bond
⊥/N , ⊥/M	∧ or circle as above	the reactions⊖ examples of . .	insert or substitute dash indicated
(/)	∧ or circle as above	bp 212 °C ∧5 kPa∧ . . .	insert or substitute parentheses
[/]	∧ or circle as above	bicyclo-∧2.2.2∧octane . .	insert or substitute brackets
{/}	∧ or circle as above	∧^{1}H∧ . . .	insert or substitute braces
!	∧ or circle as above	finished∧	insert or substitute exclamation point
?	∧ or circle as above	Are the results final⊙	insert or substitute question mark

Position

fl l	⌐	[Table I: Reaction of Amine Thiols . .	do not indent (flush left)
⌐	[	the solution [·was allowed . . .	move to left
fl r	⌐	Received January‿ 3, 1978; revised⌐	bring to right margin

Table IV (Continued)

mark in margin	mark in proof	example	meaning
⌐	⌐	Calcd for the R isomer . . .	move to right
ctr	⌐ ⌐	Scheme I	center material within margin or column indicated
⌐	⌐	C$_a$Cl$_2$ . . .	move up
⌐	⌐	per ⌐mole⌐ of . .	lower
═	═	some material was eluted at . .	straighten
‖	‖	Johnson Jones Kirdan	align
tr	∿	Arabic with numerals . .	transpose material
¶	¶	¶A paper must contain . .	begin a paragraph
no ¶	⌐	a title.⌐ In addition. .	no paragraph

Spacing

⌒	⌒	for the methyl benzene	remove space
#	| or ∧ between characters	methyl acetyl-enecarboxylate . .	insert space
eq #	∧∧	the ∧first∧ed-ition of the . .	use equal space
thin #	| between characters	at 1300 cm^{-1}32	insert thin space

Table IV (Continued)

mark in margin	mark in proof	example	meaning
		Insertion and Deletion	
ℒ	line through character(s)	glacial ~~and~~ acetic acid . .	take out
ℒ	line through character(s) and ⌒	de~~s~~siccator . .	take out and close up
character ∧ or word		occasionally a∧must be added . . .	insert at this point
stet	. . . under character(s)	the ~~proton~~ magnetic reso- nance spectra . .	do not remove

CORRECTIONS

Corrections for a paper that has already been published should be sent in duplicate to the editor or managing editor of the journal. Most American Chemical Society journals publish corrections soon after they have been received. A few print them once a year, in a December issue.

If authors observe errors immediately after the journal has been issued and notify the Editorial Department promptly, any reprints ordered may be able to be corrected. When corrections are possible, the corrected reprint will serve as the master from which the microfilm version of the journal is prepared.

REPRINTS

If reprints are desired, they should be ordered when the corrected proof is returned. The order form that is included with the proof should be completed and returned as directed thereon. A purchase order, if demanded by the author's institution, should be submitted with the order. Any purchase order submitted without the reprint order form provided by the book or journal must include adequate identification: name of book or journal, authors' names, title of article, tentative publication date.

It is possible to purchase reprints after the journal has been printed. However, the rates quoted on the reprint order form are not applicable for late orders, and all such orders should be directed to Business Operations, Books and Journals Division.

PAGE CHARGES

A form for the certification of page charge is also enclosed with the galley proofs for the following journals: *Biochemistry, Industrial & Engineering Chemistry Fundamentals, Industrial & Engineering Chemistry Process Design and Development, Industrial & Engineering Chemistry Product Research and Development, Inorganic Chemistry, Journal of Agricultural and Food Chemistry, Journal of the American Chemical Society, Journal of Chemical and Engineering Data, Journal of Chemical Information and Computer Sciences, Journal of Medicinal Chemistry, The Journal of Organic Chemistry, The Journal of Physical Chemistry,* and *Macromolecules.* The page charge is a publication service charge designed to cover some of the costs of publishing an article. Industry, government, and university administrators generally accept the page charge as a research expense, and funds are usually made available by the author's employer or by the sponsor of his research. Payment is not a condition for publication; editors and reviewers have no knowledge of who has paid since page charge payments are handled independently, after the decision to accept has been made.

After a paper is accepted, the editor will send the author a form to be completed if the author (a) intends to request the page charge be waived or (b) requires prebilling, either for page charge or for reprints or for both, because of grant expirations before normal billing (approximately 1 month after publication date).

LIABILITY AND COPYING RIGHTS

Authors are solely responsible for the accuracy of their contributions. The Society and the editors assume no responsibility for the statements and opinions advanced by the contributors to these publications.

Contributions that have appeared or have been accepted for publication with essentially the same content in another journal or in some freely available printed work (e.g., government publications, proceedings) will not be published in the Society journals. This restriction does not apply to results previously published as communications to the editor in the same or other journals.

Under the terms of the Federal copyright law, effective January 1, 1978, scientific publishers who wish to obtain copyright ownership of papers published in their journals are required specifically to obtain such ownership from the author of each paper. Since it is necessary for the widest possible dissemination of scientific knowledge that the Society own the copyright, authors are required to transfer copyright ownership before publication of their manuscript. A form for this purpose is provided to the author at the time of acknowledgment of receipt of the manuscript. A letter explaining which rights are customarily returned to authors is also provided. Works of the U.S. government are not subject to U.S. copyright.

Manuscripts published in one of the Society's books or journals and copyright to the Society may not be reprinted elsewhere without written permission from both the Society and the authors. Authors who wish to reproduce their articles for commercial use elsewhere also must have the consent of the Society. Other reproduction, except as specified in the letter to authors referred to in the preceding paragraph, is permitted only after obtaining the written consent of the Society. Requests should be addressed to Office of the Director, Books and Journals Division, at the address below.

The Society does not require a publication release for papers presented at its national or other meetings. Authors are free to submit these papers for publication wherever they desire.

Correspondence regarding reprints, page charges, copyrights, and additional information on the Society books and journals should be sent to Books and Journals Division, American Chemical Society, 1155 Sixteenth Street, N.W., Washington, D.C. 20036.

V. APPENDIXES

Appendix A: International System of Units (SI)

The great advantage of SI is that there is one and only one unit for each physical quantity. From these elemental units, units for all other quantities are derived by simple equations.

The seven base units and two supplementary units in SI, and their definitions, are given in Table V.

Derived units are formed by combining base units, supplementary units, and other derived units according to the mathematical relations linking the corresponding quantities. For example, the SI unit for area is square meter (area = length times length; $m^2 = m \times m$), and the SI unit for molar entropy is joule per mole kelvin [$J/(mol \cdot K)$]. The common derived units of SI, expressed in terms of base units and in terms of derived units and base units, are given in Table VI. Definitions of derived units having special names are given in Table VII.

Table VIII lists units in use with, but not part of, the International System. No attempt will be made to discourage the use of these units in the American Chemical Society books and journals program.

Table IX contains a list of units not part of SI that may be permitted for a limited period, depending upon particular journal or book instructions, but whose continued use is deprecated. Eventual elimination of these units is recommended, and authors are encouraged to adopt this recommendation immediately.

The National Bureau of Standards and the American National Metric Council offer guidance and give recommendations on conversion to SI. The American National Standards Institute, with joint sponsorship of the American Society for Testing and Materials and the Institute of Electrical and Electronics Engineers, has published the standard, "Metric Practice" (ANSI Z210.1-1976, IEEE Std 268-1976, ASTM E 380-76), which describes SI and its units, gives guidance on the application of the system, and provides an extensive table of conversion factors. Another useful publication is "Guidance for Using the Metric System, SI Version" (Antoine, V. Society for Technical Communication: Washington, D.C., 1976).

Table V: SI Base and Supplementary Units

physical quantity	unit	definition
length	meter	the length equal to 1 650 763.73 wavelengths in vacuum of the radiation corresponding to the transition between the levels $2p_{10}$ and $5d_5$ of the krypton-86 atom (adopted by 11th CGPM 1960)
mass	kilogram	the unit of mass; it is equal to the mass of the international prototype of the kilogram (adopted by 1st and 3rd CGPM 1889 and 1901)
time	second	the duration of 9 192 631 770 periods of the radiation corresponding to the transition between the two hyperfine levels of the ground state of the cesium-133 atom (adopted by 13th CGPM 1967)
current	ampere	that constant current which, if maintained in two straight parallel conductors of infinite length, of negligible circular cross section, and placed one meter apart in vacuum, would produce between these conductors a force equal to 2×10^{-7} newton per meter of length (adopted by 9th CGPM 1948)
temperature	kelvin	unit of thermodynamic temperature, the fraction 1/273.16 of the thermodynamic temperature of the triple point of water (adopted by 13th CGPM 1967)
amount of substance	mole	the amount of substance of a system which contains as many elementary entities as there are atoms in 0.012 kilogram of carbon-12 (adopted by 14th CGPM 1971). NOTE: When the mole is used, the elementary entities must be specified and may be atoms, molecules, ions, electrons, other particles, or specified groups of such particles.
luminous intensity	candela	the luminous intensity, in the perpendicular direction, of a surface of 1/600 000 square meter of blackbody at the temperature of freezing platinum under a pressure of 101 325 newtons per square meter (adopted by 13th CGPM 1967)
plane angle	radian	the plane angle between two radii of a circle which cut off on the circumference an arc equal in length to the radius
solid angle	steradian	the solid angle which, having its vertex in the center of a sphere, cuts off an area of the surface of the sphere equal to that of a square with sides of length equal to the radius of the sphere

Table VI: SI Derived Units[a]

quantity	name	symbol	expression in terms of other units	expression in terms of SI base units
A. SI Derived Units				
area	square meter	m^2		
volume	cubic meter	m^3		
speed, velocity	meter per second	m/s		
acceleration	meter per second squared	m/s^2		
wavenumber	one per meter	m^{-1}		
density, mass	kilogram per cubic meter	kg/m^3		
current density	ampere per square meter	A/m^2		
magnetic field strength	ampere per meter	A/m		
concentration (of amount of substance)	mole per cubic meter[b]	mol/m^3		
specific volume	cubic meter per kilogram	m^3/kg		
luminance	candela per square meter	cd/m^2		
B. SI Derived Units with Special Names				
frequency	hertz	Hz		s^{-1}
force	newton	N		$m \cdot kg \cdot s^{-2}$ [a]
pressure, stress	pascal	Pa	N/m^2	$m^{-1} \cdot kg \cdot s^{-2}$
energy, work, quantity of heat	joule	J	$N \cdot m$	$m^2 \cdot kg \cdot s^{-2}$
power, radiant flux	watt	W	J/s	$m^2 \cdot kg \cdot s^{-3}$
quantity of electricity, electric charge	coulomb	C	$A \cdot s$	$s \cdot A$
electric potential, potential difference, electromotive force	volt	V	W/A	$m^2 \cdot kg \cdot s^{-3} \cdot A^{-1}$
capacitance	farad	F	C/V	$m^{-2} \cdot kg^{-1} \cdot s^4 \cdot A^2$

Table VI (Continued)

quantity	name	symbol	expression in terms of other units	expression in terms of SI base units
electric resistance	ohm	Ω	V/A	$m^2 \cdot kg \cdot s^{-3} \cdot A^{-2}$
conductance	siemens	S	A/V	$m^{-2} \cdot kg^{-1} \cdot s^3 \cdot A^2$
magnetic flux	weber	Wb	V·s	$m^2 \cdot kg \cdot s^{-2} \cdot A^{-1}$
magnetic flux density	tesla	T	Wb/m^2	$kg \cdot s^{-2} \cdot A^{-1}$
inductance	henry	H	Wb/A	$m^2 \cdot kg \cdot s^{-2} \cdot A^{-2}$
luminous flux	lumen	lm		$cd \cdot sr$
illuminance	lux	lx	lm/m^2	$m^{-2} \cdot cd \cdot sr$
activity (radioactive)	becquerel	Bq		s^{-1}
absorbed dose	gray	Gy	J/kg	$m^2 \cdot s^{-2}$

quantity	name	symbol	expression in terms of SI base units

C. SI Derived Units Expressed by Special Names

quantity	name	symbol	expression in terms of SI base units
dynamic viscosity	pascal second	Pa·s	$m^{-1} \cdot kg \cdot s^{-1}$
moment of force	newton meter	N·m	$m^2 \cdot kg \cdot s^{-2}$
surface tension	newton per meter	N/m	$kg \cdot s^{-2}$
heat flux density, irradiance	watt per square meter	W/m^2	$kg \cdot s^{-3}$
heat capacity, entropy	joule per kelvin	J/K	$m^2 \cdot kg \cdot s^{-2} \cdot K^{-1}$
specific heat capacity, specific entropy	joule per kilogram kelvin	J/(kg·K)	$m^2 \cdot s^{-2} \cdot K^{-1}$
specific energy	joule per kilogram	J/kg	$m^2 \cdot s^{-2}$
thermal conductivity	watt per meter kelvin	W/(m·K)	$m \cdot kg \cdot s^{-3} \cdot K^{-1}$
energy density	joule per cubic meter	J/m^3	$m^{-1} \cdot kg \cdot s^{-2}$
electric field strength	volt per meter	V/m	$m \cdot kg \cdot s^{-3} \cdot A^{-1}$
electric charge density	coulomb per cubic meter	C/m^3	$m^{-3} \cdot s \cdot A$
electric flux density	coulomb per square meter	C/m^2	$m^{-2} \cdot s \cdot A$
permittivity	farad per meter	F/m	$m^{-3} \cdot kg^{-1} \cdot s^4 \cdot A^2$
permeability	henry per meter	H/m	$m \cdot kg \cdot s^{-2} \cdot A^{-2}$
molar energy	joule per mole	J/mol	$m^2 \cdot kg \cdot s^{-2} \cdot mol^{-1}$
molar entropy, molar heat capacity	joule per mole kelvin	J/(mol·K)	$m^2 \cdot kg \cdot s^{-2} \cdot K^{-1} \cdot mol^{-1}$

[a] Symbols for compound units are shown with center dots. [b] M will be retained as a special symbol for concentration of amount of substance, mole per cubic decimeter (mole per liter).

Table VII: Derived Units of the International System Having Special Names

physical quantity	unit	definition
absorbed dose	gray	the absorbed dose when one joule of energy is imparted to one kilogram of matter by ionizing radiation
activity	becquerel	the activity of a radionuclide having one spontaneous nuclear transition per second
electric capacitance	farad	the capacitance of a capacitor between the plates of which there appears a difference of potential of one volt when it is charged by a quantity of electricity equal to one coulomb
electric conductance	siemens	the electric conductance of a conductor in which a current of one ampere is produced by an electric potential difference of one volt
electric inductance	henry	the inductance of a closed circuit in which an electromotive force of one volt is produced when the electric current in the circuit varies uniformly at a rate of one ampere per second
electric potential difference, electromotive force	volt	the difference of electric potential between two points of a conductor carrying a constant current of one ampere, when the power dissipated between these points is equal to one watt
electric resistance	ohm	the electric resistance between two points of a conductor when a constant difference of potential of one volt, applied between these two points, produces in this conductor a current of one ampere, this conductor not being the source of any electromotive force
energy	joule	the work done when the point of application of a force of one newton is displaced a distance of one meter in the direction of the force
force	newton	that force which, when applied to a body having a mass of one kilogram, gives it an acceleration of one meter per second squared
frequency	hertz	the frequency of a periodic phenomenon of which the period is one second
illuminance	lux	the illuminance produced by a luminous flux of one lumen uniformly distributed over a surface of one squared meter

Table VII (Continued

physical quantity	unit	definition
luminous flux	lumen	the luminous flux emitted in a solid angle of one steradian by a point source having a uniform intensity of one candela
magnetic flux	weber	the magnetic flux which, linking a circuit of one turn, produces in it an electromotive force of one volt as it is reduced to zero at a uniform rate in one second
magnetic flux density	tesla	the magnetic flux density given by a magnetic flux of one weber per square meter
power	watt	the power which gives rise to the production of energy at the rate of one joule per second
pressure or stress	pascal	the pressure or stress of one newton per square meter
quantity of electricity	coulomb	the quantity of electricity transported in one second by a current of one ampere

Table VIII: Units in Use with SI

quantity	name	symbol	value in SI unit
A. General			
time	minute	min	$1 \text{ min} = 60 \text{ s}$
	hour	h	$1 \text{ h} = 60 \text{ min} = 3600 \text{ s}$
	day	d	$1 \text{ d} = 24 \text{ h} = 86\,400 \text{ s}$
plane angle	degree	°	$1° = (\pi/180) \text{ rad}$
	minute	′	$1' = (1/60)° = (\pi/10\,800) \text{ rad}$
	second	″	$1'' = (1/60)' = \pi/648\,000) \text{ rad}$
volume	liter	L	$1 \text{ L} = 1 \text{ dm}^3 = 10^{-3} \text{ m}^3$
mass	metric ton	t	$1 \text{ t} = 10^3 \text{ kg}$
temperature	degree Celsius	°C	a
B. Limited			
energy	kilowatt-hour	kWh	$1 \text{ kWh} = 3.6 \text{ MJ}$
area	barn	b	$1 \text{ b} = 10^{-28} \text{ m}^2$
	hectare	ha	$1 \text{ ha} = 1 \text{ hm}^2 = 10^4 \text{ m}^2$
pressure	bar	bar	$1 \text{ bar} = 10^5 \text{ Pa}$
activity	curie	Ci	$1 \text{ Ci} = 3.7 \times 10^{10} \text{ Bq}$
exposure	roentgen	R	$1 \text{ R} = 2.58 \times 10^{-4} \text{ C/kg}$
absorbed dose	rad	rd	$1 \text{ rd} = 0.01 \text{ Gy}$

a Temperature intervals in kelvin and degrees Celsius are identical; however, temperature in kelvins equals temperature in degrees Celsius plus 273.15.

Table IX: Non-SI Units That Should Be Discouraged

name	value in SI units
ångström	0.1 nm
kilogram-force	9.80665 N
calorie (thermochemical)	4.184 J
mho	1 S
standard atmosphere	101.325 kPa
technical atmosphere	98.0665 kPa
conventional millimeter of mercury	133.322 Pa
torr	133.322 Pa
grad	$2\pi/400$ rad
metric carat	0.2 g
metric horsepower	735.499 W
micron	$1 \mu m$

Appendix B: Symbols for Chemical Elements and Physicochemical Quantities

A list of the elements, their symbols, and their atomic weights is given in Table X.

A complete list of symbols for physicochemical quantities is found in "Manual of Symbols and Terminology for Physicochemical Quantities and Units", Butterworths: London, 1975. The symbols in this appendix are extracted from that list and are those most frequently encountered in American Chemical Society books and journals. Symbols separated by commas represent equivalent recommendations. Whenever possible, symbols used in a paper should follow these recommendations. If a different symbol must be used, the ad hoc representation must be carefully defined.

Space, time, and related quantities

length	l
height	h
radius	r
diameter	d
path, length of arc	s
wavelength	λ
wavenumber: $1/\lambda$	$\sigma, \tilde{\nu}$
plane angle	$\alpha, \beta, \gamma, \theta, \phi$
solid angle	ω, Ω
area	A, S

volume	V
time	t
frequency	ν, f
acceleration of free fall	g
velocity	v

Mechanical and related quantities

mass	m
reduced mass	μ
specific volume (volume divided by mass)	v
density (mass divided by volume)	ρ
relative density (ratio of the density to that of a reference substance)	d
moment of inertia	I
momentum	p
force	F
pressure	p, P
viscosity	$\eta \, (\mu)$

Molecular and related quantities

relative atomic mass of an element (also called atomic weight)	A_r
relative molecular mass of a substance (also called molecular weight)	M_r
molar mass (mass divided by amount of substance)	M
molality of solute substance B (amount of B divided by mass of solvent)	m_B

Thermodynamic and related quantities

thermodynamic temperature, absolute temperature	T
Celsius temperature	t, θ
(molar) gas constant	R
Boltzmann constant	k
heat	q, Q
work	w, W
enthalpy	H
entropy	S
Helmholtz energy	A
Gibbs energy: $H - TS$	G
heat capacity	C
specific heat capacity (heat capacity divided by mass; the name specific heat is not recommended)	c

Table X: Elements

name	symbol	atomic number	atomic weight
Actinium	Ac	89	..
Aluminum	Al	13	26.98154
Americium	Am	95	..
Antimony	Sb	51	121.75
Argon	Ar	18	39.948
Arsenic	As	33	74.9216
Astatine	At	85	..
Barium	Ba	56	137.34
Berkelium	Bk	97	..
Beryllium	Be	4	9.01218
Bismuth	Bi	83	208.9804
Boron	B	5	10.81
Bromine	Br	35	79.904
Cadmium	Cd	48	112.40
Calcium	Ca	20	40.08
Californium	Cf	98	..
Carbon	C	6	12.011
Cerium	Ce	58	140.12
Cesium	Cs	55	132.9054
Chlorine	Cl	17	35.453
Chromium	Cr	24	51.996
Cobalt	Co	27	59.9332
Copper (Cuprum)	Cu	29	63.546
Curium	Cm	96	..
Dysprosium	Dy	66	162.50
Einsteinium	Es	99	..
Erbium	Er	68	167.26
Europium	Eu	63	151.96
Fermium	Fm	100	..
Fluorine	F	9	18.99840
Francium	Fr	87	..
Gadolinium	Gd	64	157.25
Gallium	Ga	31	69.72
Germanium	Ge	32	72.59
Gold (Aurum)	Au	79	196.9665
Hafnium	Hf	72	178.49
Helium	He	2	4.00260
Holmium	Ho	67	164.9304
Hydrogen	H	1	1.0079
Indium	In	49	114.82
Iodine	I	53	126.9045
Iridium	Ir	77	192.22
Iron (Ferrum)	Fe	26	55.847
Krypton	Kr	36	83.80
Lanthanum	La	57	138.9055
Lawrencium	Lr	103	..
Lead (Plumbum)	Pb	82	207.2
Lithium	Li	3	6.941
Lutetium	Lu	71	174.97
Magnesium	Mg	12	24.305
Manganese	Mn	25	54.9380
Mendelevium	Md	101	..

Table X (Continued)

name	symbol	atomic number	atomic weight
Mercury	Hg	80	200.59
Molybdenum	Mo	42	95.94
Neodymium	Nd	60	144.24
Neon	Ne	10	20.179
Neptunium	Np	93	..
Nickel	Ni	28	58.71
Niobium	Nb	41	92.9064
Nitrogen	N	7	14.0067
Nobelium	No	102	..
Osmium	Os	76	190.2
Oxygen	O	8	15.9994
Palladium	Pd	46	106.4
Phosphorus	P	15	30.97376
Platinum	Pt	78	195.09
Plutonium	Pu	94	..
Polonium	Po	84	..
Potassium	K	19	39.098
Praseodymium	Pr	59	140.9077
Promethium	Pm	61	..
Protactinium	Pa	91	..
Radium	Ra	88	..
Radon	Rn	86	..
Rhenium	Re	75	186.2
Rhodium	Rh	45	102.9055
Rubidium	Rb	37	85.4678
Ruthenium	Ru	44	101.07
Samarium	Sm	62	150.4
Scandium	Sc	21	44.9559
Selenium	Se	34	78.96
Silicon	Si	14	28.086
Silver (Argentum)	Ag	47	107.868
Sodium	Na	11	22.98977
Strontium	Sr	38	87.62
Sulfur	S	16	32.06
Tantalum	Ta	73	180.9479
Technetium	Tc	43	..
Tellurium	Te	52	127.60
Terbium	Tb	65	158.9254
Thallium	Tl	81	204.37
Thorium	Th	90	232.0381
Thulium	Tm	69	168.9342
Tin (Stannum)	Sn	50	118.69
Titanium	Ti	22	47.90
Tungsten (Wolfram)	W	74	183.85
Uranium	U	92	238.029
Vanadium	V	23	50.9414
Xenon	Xe	54	131.30
Ytterbium	Yb	70	173.04
Yttrium	Y	39	88.9059
Zinc	Zn	30	65.38
Zirconium	Zr	40	91.22

Light and related electromagnetic radiation

Planck constant	h
Planck constant divided by 2π	$\hbar$
quantum yield	Φ
velocity of light in vacuo	c
refractive index (of a nonabsorbing material)	n
molar refraction	R_m
angle of optical rotation	α

Electricity and magnetism

elementary charge (of a proton)	e
magnetic field strength	H
Bohr magneton	μ_B
nuclear magneton	μ_N

Appendix C: Preferred Spelling

Many words in regular usage, as well as many technical terms, have two or more acceptable spellings. Within one paper, consistency is essential; within one book or journal, a uniform practice is recommended; within all the society's books and journals, a well-defined policy is desirable.

The following list gives recommended spellings, including capitalization where appropriate; included are some terms not found in easily accessible dictionaries, words often misspelled, and common expressions.

absorbance
absorbency
aerobic
aging
aglycon
air-dried (adj)
air-dry (verb)
amine (RNH_2)
ammine (NH_3 complex)
ampule
analogue
antioxidant
aqua regia

artifact
asymmetry
audio frequency
autoxidation
Avogadro

back-bonding
back-donation
backscattering
back-titrate (v)
band-pass
bandwidth
base line

Beckmann
  (rearrangement;
  thermometer)
Beilstein
bit
blackbody
black box
Bragg scattering
break-seal
Büchner
buildup (noun)
build up (verb)
buret
butanol, 1-butanol
  (not *n*-butanol)
tert-butylation
bypass
byproduct
byte

canceled
Cartesian
catalog
clear-cut
coauthor
co-ion
collinear
condensable
conductometric
conrotatory
coordination
coulombic
counterion
co-worker
cross-link
cross section
cuboctahedron
cuvette

data base
deamino
deoxy
desiccator
deuterated

deuterio
deuteroporphyrin
Dewar benzene
dialogue
disc (electrophoresis)
discernible
disk
disrotatory
dissymmetric
distill
drybox
dry ice

eigenfunction
eigenvalue
electronvolt
electron microscope
eluant
eluate
enzymatic
Erlenmeyer

far-infrared
filterable
first-order reaction
flavin
formulas
forward
free-radical reaction
freeze-dry (verb)
fulfill

gage (technical)
Gaussian
gegenion
glovebag
glovebox
Gram-positive
gray

half-life
halftone
Hamiltonian
heat-treat (v)

hemoglobin
hemolysate
homogeneous
homologue
hydrindan
hydiodide
hydrolysate
hydrolyzed
hydroxylapatite

icosahedron
indan
indexes
indices (crystallography)
inflection
in vacuo
isooctane
isosbestic

Kékulé
Kjeldahl

labeled
least squares (noun)
least-squares analysis
leukocyte
leveling
levorotatory
lifetime
ligancy
line width
liquefy
lysed

makeup (noun)
Markownikoff
metalation
methyl Cellosolve
methyl orange
midpoint
Millipore
mixture melting point
Mössbauer

nearest-neighbor (adj)
near-ultraviolet

ortho ester
orthoformate
outgassing
overall

parametrization
path length
percent
pharmacopeia
phlorin
phosphomonoester
phosphorus
1-piperidinyloxy
pipet
2-propanol (not isopropanol)
pseudo first order
pseudo-first-order reaction
pyrolysate

quantitation

radioelement
radio frequency
radioiodine
reexamine
reform (to amend)
re-form (to form again)
riboflavin
ring-expand (verb)
rotamer

sideband
side chain
spin-label (noun)
steam-distill (verb)
stereopair
superacid
superhigh frequency
sulfur
syndet
syrup

test tube

thermostated

theta solvent

thiamin

thio acid

thioether

toward

transmetalation

tropin

ultrahigh

un-ionized

uni-univalent

upfield

urethane

VandenHeuvel

van der Waals

van't Hoff–Le Bel

voltametric

voltammetric

wave function

wavelength

wavenumber

well-known

work up (verb)

workup (noun)

X irradiation

X-ray

X-ray (adj)

X-ray (verb)

ylide

Appendix D: Recurring Errors

The first edition of the American Chemical Society "Handbook for Authors" contained a section on grammatical errors. Since these are duplicated in books on grammar and style (Skillin and Gay, "Words into type", for example), only those mistakes that are especially common in the Society's books and journals program are discussed here. In addition, Society practice that differs from previous style is noted.

Papers submitted for publication by the American Chemical Society have four principal recurring grammatical errors: subjects and verbs that disagree in number, misplaced modifiers, incorrect punctuation, and poor sentence construction. Examples of these can be found in almost every publication.

The following examples illustrate incorrect usage. The changes in the margin serve a twofold purpose: to point out the errors, and to indicate how corrections should be marked on galley proof.

A. Incorrect Number. This category includes disagreement of simple subject and verb, of compound subject and verb, of compound sentences in which the number of the auxiliary verb form changes and the auxiliary must therefore be stated, and of the verb form with collective nouns (collective nouns are also discussed under Changes in Style).

(a) Assignments of the coordination site was made   ƒ
     on the basis of spectral similarities.

(b) Growth and isolation of M13 virus ~~has~~ been de-
     scribed. Preparation of antiserum to M13 coat
     protein, affinity purification of the antibody by
     combination with virus, and isolation of goat

antibody to rabbit γ-globulin ~~was~~ studied by pre- ∧ *were*
viously published methods.

(c) The lysates were centrifuged to equilibrium in
CsCl and the distribution of [^{121}I]Ig determined by ∧ *was*
immunoprecipitation.

(d) The series ~~have~~ been arranged in order of de- *has*
creasing nuclear size.

B. Misplaced Modifiers. The principal examples of poor usage under
this category are dangling introductory phrases, clauses, and partic-
iples.

∧ Pursu~~ing~~ the conformational homology indicated   ∧ *We lc* ∧ *∼e*
by the X-ray data of Vainstine et al. (1975), the   ∧ *and concluded*
functional replacement of Trp A12 between helices
A and E may well weaken the strength of interaction between the E helix and the heme group.

After ~~carefully stirring~~ the interphase, nuclei were   *was carefully*
pelleted by centrifugation.   *stirred*

C. Incorrect Punctuation. This is too broad a category to discuss in
detail. Three recurring types of misuse are prevalent in Society publications: interior phrases set off by only one comma, semicolons used to
separate subordinate clauses from main clause (although and whereas
phrases are often victims), and restrictive clauses treated as nonre-
strictive.

(a) An improved form of the Leviel equation, derived
by Newman should be used, and simplified means   ∧
of calculation are available.

(b) The dn/dc values for a large number of proteins
are within about 5% of 0.190, suggesting that this
parameter should be essentially independent of the
conformation of the protein under investigation   ∧
Whereas alterations in the conformation of heme   *lc*
proteins will be more strongly reflected in the absorbance parameter and the extinction values.

(c) The solid that melted at 250 °C was assumed to   *ſ ſ*
be the l isomer.

D. Poor Construction. This often results in nonsense sentences.

∧ Following the decrease in absorbance at 360 nm,   ∧ *We lc* ∧ *∼*
∧ prove$ to be the most sensitive wavelength.   ∧ *since this* .

That this can cause extensive unfolding has been
shown previously by many workers (ref 32) ~~in~~ ^ see ^ *which*
~~which~~ Mg^{2+} ~~was~~ depleted through dialysis. *S S* *ation* ^) *describes*

E. The Noun-as-Adjective Habit.

While not an error, the habit of using nouns as adjectives is so em-
bedded in the style of many writers that the practice produces unwieldy
results. Consider a title, Basic solvent radical-induced hydrogen abstraction from cyclic hydrocarbons, and compare two alternatives:
Radical-induced hydrogen abstraction from cyclic hydrocarbons in basic
solvent, and radical-induced abstraction of hydrogen from cyclic hydrocarbons in basic solvent. A good rule to follow would be: two modifiers preceding a noun are fine, three may be too many, four are more
than enough.

F. Collective Nouns.

A collective noun is a noun that is singular in form but could be used
with a plural implication. It is treated as singular or plural at discretion.
In general, the collective noun takes a singular verb when the group as
a whole is meant; a plural verb, when individuals of the group are meant.
Common collective nouns are contents, couple, data, dozen, grams,
group, majority, number, pair, series, variety.

G. Changes in Style.

(a) React:
The acceptance of the verb form react is worth mentioning:
Former prohibition: A is reacted with B.
Suggested change: A is treated with B.
                             A is allowed to react with B.
Current usage: All three forms are acceptable,
but the last one is wordy, and therefore least desirable. In addition,
active voice constructions should be used, rather than passive voice.
Thus, "A reacted with B" is a fourth, and preferable, alternative.

(b) Data: In the first edition of the handbook, data was treated as a
plural noun, requiring a plural verb. Data is now widely accepted as a
collective noun. Therefore, a singular or a plural verb form is correct,
depending upon context.

H. Special Precautions: Affect, Effect, Homogeneous

Affect is a verb form, meaning to change or modify.
Effect is primarily a noun, meaning the result of something. It can
be used as a verb, meaning to cause.
Homogeneous is one of the most commonly misspelled words in the
Society's publications, incorrectly appearing as homogenous.

Appendix E: Composition Procedures

Four composition methods are being used to produce American Chemical Society books and journals: computer-assisted photocomposition, hot metal composition, typewriter composition, and direct reproduction of author-supplied camera-ready copy. Each has distinct advantages and certain limitations. An author who is familiar with the composition techniques and their limitations will prepare a manuscript that will be easier to process, from editing through corrections and printing.

The journals of the Society use photocomposition, typewriter composition, and author-supplied camera-ready copy. The books are produced by all four methods.

Hot metal composition involves preparing characters or lines of type using molten metal (Monotype: individual characters; Linotype: in line units). Characters are limited to the matrices available, but an experienced Monotype compositor can generally produce anything called for. However, for scientific work considerable manual effort is involved, making this an expensive and time-consuming technique.

An author who is preparing a manuscript containing unusual characters and difficult notation is advised to consult with the editors on the availability of characters, and to design the paper from the list provided or the recommendations made.

Making corrections in Monotype may involve a simple juxtaposition of adjacent characters (form to from, for example), a simple procedure with little danger of additional errors' being introduced; it may also involve extensive resetting or respacing of material whenever the changes made involve more than one line of type. Linotype corrections require resetting of whole-line segments.

Typewriter composition is exactly what the name implies. Its limitations are character availability, appearance, and correction procedures. Characters not available on the various fonts (in this case, balls) have to be produced otherwise and manually pasted in on final output. Appearance deficiencies include nonjustified margins (in those of the Society's publications that use this method) and poor presentation of mathematical displays. Corrections often necessitate resetting the entire block of material (to end of paragraph) from the line in which the changes or additions are being made.

Author-prepared camera-ready copy has distinct economic advantages. However, the disadvantages include nonuniform appearance, wasted space, and, most important, underedited material, quite often replete with inconsistencies and grammatical and nomenclature errors. When camera-ready copy is used in conjunction with material that is processed by another technique, the two will often be different in treatment of similar subjects. The author who provides camera-ready copy (whether for an entire article, as in the Symposium Series, or for use in the Miniprint or Supplementary Material programs, or for structures) has a special responsibility to follow the recommendations outlined in this handbook and in the instructions for the specific book series or journal. In addition, corrections entail preparation and re-processsing of entire pieces of material.

Photocomposition is an extremely flexible technique with considerable advantages in design, format, and correction as well as data-base publishing, with many of its possible applications not yet realized. With photocomposition only material being corrected is modified by the changes made; any subsequent material will be reproduced by the equipment, with modifications only in line justification and hyphenation. The character availability is still a serious disadvantage, but this is temporary. Improved technology and extended character sets will permit a versatility never previously experienced in composition. In addition, input into the composition system is not restricted to one mode. Technology is available to permit input and processing of manuscripts submitted on magnetic tape or as copy that can be read by optical character recognition devices. However, using these media will necessitate preparations of standards and format recommendations. Development on these topics is in progress.

Appendix F: Guidelines for Preparation and Submission of Documents to be Microfilmed

American Chemical Society microforms are processed to conform to the highest industry standards; however, the quality of the finished microfiche or microfilm can be no better than the source document from which it is filmed. To produce high-quality, legible microforms, authors should observe the following guidelines.

(1) Material should be an original or a *clear* photocopy, preferably the former. If the material is a copy, it should not be hazy or have black lines running through it. All characters should be clean and legible. The paper should be clean, as new as possible, and white.

(2) Characters should be produced with black ink or ribbon on a white background. They should be large enough to be read comfortably in original form. A microfilmed document is reduced (American Chemical Society microforms use a reduction ratio of 24:1) in filming. Then it is blown up to its original size, which is most frequently 22 × 28 cm in size. This is also the average microform reader screen size.

Therefore, in determining whether the characters and text are of readable size or not, the answer lies in the source document to be microfilmed. Is it readable in its original form?

(3) The information area of the 22 × 28 cm document should not exceed 20 × 26 cm.

(4) Good spacing of characters and even line weight produce consistently good results on microfilm. Characters that are poorly spaced or formed will give poor results.

(5) The use of typing on drawings and copy in submitted supplementary material is substantial. Excellent quality for microfilming can be achieved if good equipment and ribbons are used. These points should be considered when using typewritten material:

(a) it should leave a clear, sharp impression;

(b) it should not be smudged;

(c) it should photograph well and should be on good quality paper;

(d) the typing should not penetrate the paper and should not show any erasures or corrections.

(6) Whenever possible, all characters and text in the information area should be upright and right-reading, that is, reading from left to right across the 22-cm width of the paper. Recently the ACS Microform program has been filming most material so that it can be read right-reading. However, this may cause the material to span two frames and is more expensive. Oversized material or material that is displayed on the length of the page should be used only when it cannot be presented in the standard format. This material may be cut apart in processing; submission of properly prepared material would preclude this practice and the resultant possibility of error.

(7) Edges of paper should be cut cleanly and evenly; dog-eared or torn, sloppy edges show up on microfilm.

(8) The contrast and density of all material should be adequate and of sufficient uniformity so that all information on the source document can be reproduced with such fidelity that its use will not be impaired. Contrast is a measure of the opacity between the information and background. Color, whether paper or printing, decreases contrast. Onionskin paper is not dense enough. Both colored and light-textured paper should be avoided.

(9) Do not use adhesive or other shiny tape on the surface of the document. The tape causes glare when the copy is being microfilmed.

(10) The copy to be microfilmed should be as clean and unmarked as possible. Staples will leave marks, and smudges will also reproduce. Use paper clips to keep the copy together and correction fluid to remove extraneous marks.

Appendix G: Hints to the Typist

All typing, including abstract, footnotes, tables, etc., should be double spaced, except for *ACS Symposium Series* manuscripts, which are typed single space (because of the composition procedure). Margins should be approximately 2 cm. References and notes should be in order at the end of the manuscript; they should not be typed immediately following the line in which citation to them is made. Display material should be separated from the text by a triple space below the lowest point. Because the styles of report presentation change, the manner in which items are arranged on the pages will differ for each publication. Illustrations and recommendations in Sections II and III of this handbook should be carefully followed. All symbols, Greek letters, signs, large parentheses, braces, etc., for which typewriter elements are unavailable should be traced on the copy.

When the work is not to be reproduced in quantity, white bond paper should be used. Clear, sharp copies made by a permanent duplication process are acceptable for the primary copy and are preferred, for second and third copies, to carbon copies. If it is necessary to use carbon copies, a good quality (cockle-finish) onionskin paper should be used. A good ribbon should be used. Correction tape or correction fluid is recommended for making corrections.

Chemical Symbols. Each chemical symbol representing an element is one capital letter and zero, one, or two lower case letters (*see* Appendix B for a list of elements and their symbols).

Do not add space between symbols and numbers in chemical formulas; they are typed *close* in this style:

$C_2H_2O_4$, $NaHSO_4$, $Ca(HCO_3)_2$

Add the usual space around the symbols for "plus", "equal", and "arrows" in chemical formulas.

Chemical Nomenclature. Take care in checking spelling, capitalizing, combining forms, spacing, underscoring for italics. Follow as closely as possible the style of the publication for which you are preparing the manuscript.

Position numbers precede the part of the name to which they refer and are connected to the name with hyphens. Separate two or more numbers with commas. Sometimes periods are used between bracketed numbers.

2,2-dichloropropane
2-amino-4,6-dichloropyrimidine
2,5-dichloro-2'-hydroxy-4-methylazobenzene
1-chlorobicyclo[2.2.2]octane

If a compound begins a sentence, type the first name only with an initial capital.

1-chloro-2-methyl-1-propene (within a sentence)
1-Chloro-2-methyl-1-propene (begins a sentence)

Letter abbreviations for specific prefixes and Greek letters may be combined with position numbers. Most letter abbreviations should be underscored to indicate italics. Greek letters should not be underlined.

4,5-dibromo-o-xylene
γ-aminopyridine
m-hydroxybenzaldehyde

Superscripts and Subscripts. Superscripts, also referred to as superiors or exponents, and subscripts, often called inferiors, may be single letters, Greek letters, numbers, mathematical symbols, or groups (multiple scripts) which form complex patterns.

A superscript or subscript pattern belongs specifically to a single character or to a pattern of many characters. This means that all of these script patterns are typed as closely as possible to the character or pattern to which they belong, but superscripts and subscripts that belong to the same character should not be typed directly above one another.

Single superscripts are typed slightly above the line character and single subscripts slightly below the line character. To line up all superscripts and subscripts, first type the main line leaving space for the superscripts and subscripts, then go back and type them in. There may be superscripts and subscripts *to* superscripts, and superscripts and subscripts *to* subscripts. Be careful that these extra scripts do not wander too far from the pattern to which they belong.

$$3Ca^{2+} + 2PO_4{}^{3-} \rightarrow Ca_3(PO_4)_2$$

$$K_{sp} = (\gamma_+ m_+)^a (\gamma_- m_-)^b = m_+{}^a m_-{}^b (\gamma_\pm)^{a+b}$$

$$\tilde{v}^E = (\tilde{v}^o)^{7/3} [4/3 - (\tilde{v}^o)^{1/3}]^{-1} [\tilde{T} - \tilde{T}^o]$$

In typing *thermodynamic* symbols, such as $S°_0$ and $H°_0$, use the degree sign as superscript and zero as the subscript. Remember that the scripts should not be one above the other. Never use the lower case letter o to represent the cipher zero.

Wherever possible fractions should be typed in a script pattern with the diagonal fraction bar instead of a horizontal fraction bar.

$$(2D_z)^{1/2}; \quad xy/z$$

Reaction Equations. The alignment and spacing are the same for all typed equations. The plus and the arrow have the standard space before and after. Typit key bars are available for the typing of arrows. A ruler should be used for arrows that are to be drawn.

When an equation must be carried over to a second line or more than two lines, select the arrow as the breaking point.

$$Ni(NH_2CH_2CH_2CO_2)_2 + NH_2^- \longrightarrow$$
$$[Ni(NHCH_2CH_2CO_2)(NH_2CH_2CH_2CO_2)]^- + NH_3$$

Line Bonds. An "equals" key may be used for a double bond and a hyphen for a single bond. Never space around bond lines.

Mathematical Patterns. *Equations.* The starting place in typing an equation, a fraction, or almost any pattern is called the "main line". The major symbols ($=, +, -, >, <$, etc.), the equation number, punctuation, and parentheses and brackets should be typed on this line. The required pattern is then typed either above or below this level.

Fractions. Complex fractions should be typed with a horizontal bar. The fraction bar is made with the underscore key and is exactly as long as the longer term. The smaller pattern is then centered on this fraction bar.

$$\log\left[\frac{(k_{1c}/k_{1t})_1}{(k_{1c}/k_{1t})_2}\right] = \frac{\Delta E}{2.303R}\left[\frac{1}{T_2} - \frac{1}{T_1}\right]$$

$$\frac{1}{G(H_2) - 3.4} = \frac{1}{G_{e^-solv}} + \frac{1.}{G_{e^-solv}}\frac{k_1[N_2O]}{k_9[H^+]}$$

Notations. The *summation symbol* $\sum$, the *product symbol* Π, and the *integral symbol* $\int$ may be drawn. The upper limits (above the symbol) and the lower limits (below the symbol) should be typed.

$$i_m = -i\sum_{k=1}^{m-1} \alpha_{km}V_k \qquad\qquad \prod_{k=0}^{m-1}(1 - k\frac{m}{r})$$

When the summation (or product or integral sign) appears in text paragraphs, the limits should be shifted to the *right* above and below (staggered).

$$\prod_{-\infty}^{\infty} , \quad \text{and} \quad \sum_{n=1}^{\infty}$$

Appendix H: Journal Abbreviations

References to journals should be abbreviated according to the recommendations in ISO 4-1972(E) and 833-1974(E) (*see* Format for Documentation). The following list gives abbreviations for journals frequently cited in American Chemical Society publications. Note that one-word titles are not abbreviated (*Chemistry, Nature, Science*).

Acc. Chem. Res.
Acta Crystallogr., Sect. A
Acta Crystallogr., Sect. B
Adv. Chem. Ser.
AIChE J.
AIChE Symp. Ser.
Anal. Biochem.
Anal. Chem.
Anal. Chim. Acta
Anal. Lett.
Angew. Chem.
Ann. Chim. (Paris)
Antimicrob. Agents Chemother.
Appl. Opt.
Appl. Phys. Lett.
Appl. Polym. Symp.
Appl. Spectrosc.
Arch. Biochem. Biophys.
Aust. J. Chem.

Ber. Bunsenges. Phys. Chem.
Biochem. Biophys. Res. Commun.
Biochemistry
Biochem. J.
Biochim. Biophys. Acta
Biochimie
Biofizika
Biokhimiya
Biopolymers
Bull. Chem. Soc. Jpn.
Bull. Soc. Chim. Belg.
Bull. Soc. Chim. Fr.

Cancer Chemother. Rep., Part 1
Cancer Res.
Can. J. Biochem.
Can. J. Chem.
Carbohydr. Res.
Chem. Ber.
Chem.-Biol. Interact.
Chem. Eng. News
Chem. Eng. (N.Y.)
Chem. Ind. (London)
Chem.-Ing.-Tech.
Chemistry

Chem. Lett.
Chem. Listy
Chemotherapy (Tokyo)
Chem. Pharm. Bull.
Chem. Phys.
Chem. Phys. Lett.
CHEMTECH
Chem.-Ztg.
Chim. Ind. (Milan)
Clin. Chem. (Winston-Salem, N.C.)
Cold Spring Harbor Symp. Quant. Biol.
Collect. Czech. Chem. Commun.
C. R. Acad. Sci., Ser. B

Dokl. Akad. Nauk SSSR

Electrochim. Acta
Endocrinology
Environ. Sci. Technol.
Eur. J. Biochem.
Exp. Cell Res.
Experientia

Faraday Discuss. Chem. Soc.
FEBS Lett.
Fed. Proc., Fed. Am. Soc. Exp. Biol.

Gazz. Chim. Ital.

Helv. Chim. Acta
Hoppe-Seyler's Z. Physiol. Chem.

Ind. Eng. Chem. Fundam.
Ind. Eng. Chem. Process Des. Dev.
Ind. Eng. Chem. Prod. Res. Dev.
IEEE J. Quantum Electron.
Inorg. Chem.
Inorg. Chim. Acta
Inorg. Nucl. Chem. Lett.
Int. J. Chem. Kinet.
Int. J. Mass Spectrom. Ion Phys.
Int. J. Quantum Chem.
Isr. J. Chem.
Izv. Akad. Nauk SSSR, Ser. Khim.

J. Agric. Food Chem.
J. Am. Chem. Soc.
J. Am. Oil Chem. Soc.
J. Assoc. Off. Anal. Chem.
J. Bacteriol.
J. Biochem. (Tokyo)
J. Chem. Soc., Chem. Commun.
J. Chem. Soc., Dalton Trans.
J. Chem. Soc., Faraday Trans. 1
J. Chem. Soc., Faraday Trans. 2
J. Chem. Soc., Perkin Trans. 1
J. Chem. Soc., Perkin Trans. 2
J. Chim. Phys. Phys.-Chim. Biol.
J. Chromatogr.
J. Electrochem. Soc.
J. Endocrinol.
Jerusalem Symp. Quantum Chem. Biochem.
J. Fluorine Chem.
J. Heterocycl. Chem.
J. Inorg. Nucl. Chem.
J. Lipid Res.
J. Macromol. Sci., Chem.
J. Macromol. Sci., Phys.
J. Magn. Reson.
J. Med. Chem.
J. Mol. Biol.
J. Mol. Spectrosc.
J. Organomet. Chem.
J. Org. Chem.
J. Phys. B
J. Phys. C
J. Phys. Chem.
J. Phys. Chem. Solids
J. Physiol. (London)
J. Phys. (Paris)
J. Polym. Sci., Polym. Chem. Ed.
J. Polym. Sci., Polym. Lett. Ed.
J. Polym. Sci., Polym. Phys. Ed.
J. Polym. Sci., Polym. Symp.
Justus Liebigs Ann. Chem.

Lipids

Macromolecules
Makromol. Chem.
Monatsh. Chem.

Nature (London)
Nature (London), New Biol.
Nature (London), Phys. Sci.
Naturwissenschaften

Org. Mass Spectrom.

Phys. Lett. A
Phys. Rev. A
Phys. Rev. Lett.
Polym. J.
Polym. Prepr., Am. Chem. Soc., Div. Polym. Chem.
Prepr., Div. Pet. Chem., Am. Chem. Soc.
Proc. Natl. Acad. Sci. U.S.A.
Proc. R. Soc. London, Ser. A
Proc. Soc. Exp. Biol. Med.
Pure Appl. Chem.

Recl. Trav. Chim. Pays-Bas
Rocz. Chem.

Science
Spectrochim. Acta, Part A
Spectrosc. Lett.
Steroids
Synth. Commun.

Tetrahedron
Tetrahedron Lett.
Theor. Chim. Acta

Usp. Khim.

Z. Anorg. Allg. Chem.
Zh. Fiz. Khim.
Z. Naturforsch. A
Zh. Neorg. Khim.
Zh. Obshch. Khim.
Zh. Org. Khim.
Z. Phys. Chem. (Frankfurt am Main)
Z. Phys. Chem. (Leipzig)

VI. SELECTED REFERENCES

ANSI Standards

"American National Standard for Bibliographic References", ANSI Z39.29; American National Standards Institute: New York, 1976.

"American National Standard guidelines for format and production of scientific and technical reports", ANSI Z39.18-1974; American National Standards Institute: New York, 1974.

"American National Standard metric practice", ANSI Z210.1-1976; American National Standards Institute: New York, 1976.

"American National Standard for the preparation of scientific papers for written or oral presentation", ANSI Z39.16-1972; American National Standards Institute: New York, 1972 (revision in process).

"American National Standard proof corrections", ANSI Z39.22-1974; American National Standards Institute: New York, 1974.

"American National Standard for Synoptics"; American National Standards Institute: New York (in preparation).

"American National Standard for Writing Abstracts", ANSI Z39.14-1971; American National Standards Institute: New York, 1971 (revision in process).

ISO Standards

"Documentation—International code for the abbreviation of titles of periodicals", ISO 4-1972(E); International Organization for Standardization: 1972 (American National Standards Institute, New York).

"Documentation—International list of periodical title word abbreviations", ISO 833-1974(E); International Organization for Standardization: 1974 (American National Standards Institute; New York).

"SI units and recommendations for the use of their multiples and of certain other units", ISO 1000-1973(E); International Organization for Standardization: 1973 (American National Standards Institute; New York).

Nomenclature

Banks, James E. "Naming Organic Compounds", 2nd ed.; W. B. Saunders: Philadelphia, 1976.

Cahn, R. S. "Introduction to Chemical Nomenclature", 4th ed.; Wiley: New York, 1974.

"Chemical Abstracts Service Index Guide"; Chemical Abstracts Service: Columbus, Ohio, 1978.

"Condensed Chemical Dictionary", 9th ed.; Van Nostrand-Reinhold: New York, 1977.

International Union of Pure and Applied Chemistry. "Manual of Symbols and Terminology for Physicochemical Quantities and Units"; Butterworths: London, 1965.

"Merck Index to Chemicals and Drugs"; Merck & Co.: Rahway, N.J., 1976.

"Nomenclature of Inorganic Chemistry", 2nd ed.; Butterworths: London, 1971.

"Nomenclature of Organic Chemistry, Sections A, B & C"; Butterworths: London, 1971.

"Nomenclature of Organic Chemistry, Section D, Appendices on Tentative Nomenclature, Symbols, Units, and Standards, No. 31"; International Union of Pure and Applied Chemistry: Oxford, 1973.

"Nomenclature of Organic Chemistry, Section E"; *J. Org. Chem.* **1970,** *35,* 2849.

"Nomenclature of Organic Chemistry, Section F, Appendices on Provisional Nomenclature, Symbols, Terminology, and Conventions, No. 53"; International Union of Pure and Applied Chemistry: Oxford, 1976.

"Nomenclature of Organic Compounds". Fletcher, John H.; Dermer, Otis C.; Fox, Robert B., Eds.; American Chemical Society: Washington, D.C., 1974.

"The SOCMA Handbook"; American Chemical Society: Washington, D.C., 1965 (out of print, but still useful).

"USAN and the USP dictionary of drug names", United States Pharmacopeial Convention: Rockville, Md., 1977.

SI

"American National Standard Metric Practice", ANSI Z210.1-1976; American National Standards Institute: New York, 1976.

Antoine, Valerie. "Guidance for Using the Metric System. SI Version"; Society for Technical Communication: Washington, D.C., 1975.

"The International System of Units (SI)"; Special Publication No. 330; National Bureau of Standards: Washington, D.C., 1977.

"Metric Editorial Guide", 3rd ed.; American National Metric Council: Washington, D.C., 1978.

Style Manuals

"The AOAC Style Manual"; Association of Official Analytical Chemists: Washington, D.C., 1972.

"ASTM Style Manual"; American Society for Testing and Materials: Philadelphia, 1969.

"Council of Biology Editors Style Manual", 3rd ed.; American Institute of Biological Sciences: Washington, 1978.

"Handbook and Style Manual"; American Society of Agronomy, Crop Science Society of America, and Soil Science Society of America: Madison, Wis., 1976.

"A Manual for Authors of Mathematical Papers"; American Mathematical Society: Providence, R.I., 1973.

"A Manual of Style", 12th ed., rev.; The University of Chicago Press: Chicago, 1975.

"Publication Manual of the American Psychological Association", 2nd ed.; American Psychological Association: Washington, 1974.

"Style Manual"; American Institute of Physics: New York, 1973.

Miscellaneous

Berry, T. E. "The most common mistakes in English"; McGraw-Hill: New York, 1961.

Bernstein, T. M. "The Careful Writer: A Modern Guide to English Usage"; Atheneum: New York, 1965.

"Bibliographic Guide for Editors & Authors"; American Chemical Society: Washington, D.C., 1974.

"Chemical Abstracts Service Source Index, 1907–1974 Cumulative"; Chemical Abstracts Service: Columbus, Ohio, 1975.

Clements, W.; Berb, R.; "The Scientific Report: A Guide for Authors"; University of California: Livermore, 1969.

Evans, B.; Evans, C. "A Dictionary of Contemporary American Usage", Random House: New York, 1957.

Fowler, H. W. "A Dictionary of Modern English Usage", 2nd ed.; Oxford University Press: New York, 1965.

Hawley, G. G.; Hawley, A. W.; compilers. "The Technical Speller"; Reinhold; New York, 1964.

Hodges, J. C.; Whitten, M. E. "Harbrace College Handbook", 8th ed.; Harcourt, Brace, Jovanovich: New York, 1977.

"Instructions for the use of the stencil for drawing organic structural formulas" and "Formula. Stencil II. Stereochemistry"; Verlag Chemie: Weinheim, 1975.

Nicholson, M. "Dictionary of American-English Usage"; Oxford University Press: New York, 1965.

O'Connor, M.; Woodford, F. P. "Writing Scientific Papers in English: An Else-Ciba Foundation Guide for Authors"; Elsevier, Excerpta Medica: North-Holland, 1975.

Perrin, P. G. "Writer's Guide and Index to English", 4th ed.; Scott, Foresman & Co.: Glenview, Ill., 1968.

Riebel, J. P. "How to write Reports, Papers, Theses, Articles"; Arco Publishing Co.: New York, 1972.

Skillin, M. E.; Gay, R. M. "Words into type", 3rd ed.; Prentice-Hall, Englewood Cliffs, N.J., 1974.

Strunk, W. S., Jr.; White, E. B. "Elements of Style"; Macmillan: New York, 1972.

Swanson, E. "Mathematics into Type"; American Mathematical Society: Providence, R.I., 1971.

"Thomas Register of American Manufacturers and Thomas Register Catalog File"; Thomas Publishing Co.: New York: 1976.

Tichy, H. J. "Effective Writing for engineers, managers, scientists"; Wiley: New York, 1966.

Velte, C. "The Treatment of Technical Names". *Tech. Commun.* **1975,** (3), 6–8.

"Websters Third New International Dictionary of the English Language"; G. & C. Merriam: Springfield, Mass., 1965.

"Webster's New World Dictionary of the American Language", 2nd College ed.; Collins-World: Cleveland, Ohio, 1976.

Weisman, H. M. "Technical Report Writing"; Charles E. Merrill: Columbus, Ohio, 1975.

Index